CONTENTS

6 Foreword by Paul Di Filippo

9 Introduction

10 Maker's Workshop

18 Basic Jewelry-Making Techniques

22 **PROJECTS AND SIDES**

22 Filigree Gears Necklace

26 Sidebar: Steampunk Roots

28 The Anachronist Necklace

32 Sidebar: Sci-Fi Origins

34 Captured Time Ring

38 Sidebar: Modding

40 Rubies in Time Bracelet

43 Sidebar: The Community

44 Love's Labour's Lost Ensemble

48 Sidebar: Topping It Off

50 Gearrings

53 Sidebar: About Lolita

54 Minerva's Folly Cuff

58 Sidebar: Dressing Up

60 Portal Explorers Necklace

64 Sidebar: Gear

Steampunk-Style JEWELRY

First published in the United States of America by
Creative Publishing international, Inc., a member of
Quayside Publishing Group
400 First Avenue North, Suite 300, Minneapolis, MN 55401
1-800-328-3895
www.creativepub.com

Visit www.Craftside.Typepad.com
for a behind-the-scenes peek at our crafty world!

ISBN-13: 978-1-58923-475-8
ISBN-10: 1-58923-475-8

10 9 8 7 6

Library of Congress Cataloging-in-Publication Data

Campbell, Jean, 1964-
  Steampunk-style jewelry : a maker's collection of Victorian, fantasy, and
mechanical designs / Jean Campbell.
    p. cm.
  Includes index.
  ISBN-13: 978-1-58923-475-8
  ISBN-10: 1-58923-475-8
  1. Jewelry making. I. Title.

  TT212.C335 2010
  739.27—dc22

                    2009031408

Technical Editor: Judith Durant
Copy Editor: Tamara Honaman
Book & Cover Design: Laura H. Couallier, Laura Herrmann Design
Illustrations: Julia S. Pretl
Photographs: All photographs by Glenn Scott unless otherwise noted.

Printed in China

Steampunk-Style JEWELRY

VICTORIAN, FANTASY, AND MECHANICAL
NECKLACES, BRACELETS, AND EARRINGS

Jean Campbell

Creative Publishing
international

66 Time Traveler's Necklace
70 Sidebar: 2-D Steampunk

72 White Star Line Necklace
76 Sidebar: Steampunk Sound

78 Steam Voyageur Necklace
83 Sidebar: Steampunk on Stage

84 Machinery in Motion Necklace
88 Sidebar: At the Movies

90 Horological Faery Gadget Necklace
94 Sidebar: Steampunk Animated

96 Airship Captain's Ring
100 Sidebar: The Spirit of Play

102 Dirigible Aviatrix Necklace
107 Sidebar: Green Steam

108 Voluminating Exhalator Bracelet
112 Sidebar: Choosing Materials

114 Chronos #8 Necklace
118 Sidebar: Steampunk Sculpture

120 Tick Tock Drop Earrings
123 Sidebar: Steampunk Couture

124 Tempus Fugit Pendant
128 Sidebar: Goggles Galore

130 Admiral's Secret Cuff

134 GALLERY OF STEAMPUNK DESIGNS

142 List of Artists
143 Credits
144 Supplies

These pages: *Handmade Steampunk Unisex and Diverse Vintage Neo-Victorian Jewelry*
Ricky Wolbrom, EDM Designs

Foreword

Anachronistic Futures of Elegant Tech

Surely you've heard the saying, "It's never too late to have a happy childhood." The exploding cultural wavefront known as Steampunk might very well adopt as its motto, "It's never too late to live splendidly like a Victorian."

But, of course, just as no sane adult seeks to replicate exactly all the cramped and shortsighted parameters of childhood, so no thoughtful creator or lifestyle adopter seeks to authentically inhabit the constricted and narrow-minded conditions of 150 years ago.

Steampunk takes the best of this seminal historical mother lode and mixes it up with postmodern influences that range from attitude to materials. We Steampunks are bricoleurs, with one foot set firmly in the Victorian era and the other solidly planted in the twenty-first century, yoking the elegance and brio of the past with the ineluctable concerns and visions of the future.

"Steam" plus "punk." That's the ticket!

The type of antique things and techniques the Steampunk artist or recreationist instinctively seeks and utilizes are those objects and technics for which the current period offers only inferior or ugly or distasteful counterparts. Cast-iron and wood instead of aluminum. Silk and linen instead of polyester. Brass and glass and rubber instead of plastic. Welding instead of superglue. Rivets instead of injection molding. Leather belts and buckles instead of Velcro. Decoration instead of utilitarianism. Irony and humor instead of severity and starkness.

The Steampunk artisan always favors rich, beautiful materials and painstaking artisanal methods that hark back to a less recondite and less machine-mediated technology, when natural resources emerged transmogrified but still recognizable from the workshop and factory.

And, most important, Steampunk cultivates a DIY ethos, in line with the fabled music from which half its name derives. The Victorian and Edwardian era represented the last period in which broad expertise and knowledge were obtainable by the average person, even if self-taught. It was a time when every woman could be her own jungle explorer, every man his own

Steampunk-Style JEWELRY

First published in the United States of America by
Creative Publishing international, Inc., a member of
Quayside Publishing Group
400 First Avenue North, Suite 300, Minneapolis, MN 55401
1-800-328-3895
www.creativepub.com

Visit www.Craftside.Typepad.com
for a behind-the-scenes peek at our crafty world!

ISBN-13: 978-1-58923-475-8
ISBN-10: 1-58923-475-8

10 9 8 7 6

Library of Congress Cataloging-in-Publication Data

Campbell, Jean, 1964-
  Steampunk-style jewelry : a maker's collection of Victorian, fantasy, and mechanical designs / Jean Campbell.
     p. cm.
  Includes index.
  ISBN-13: 978-1-58923-475-8
  ISBN-10: 1-58923-475-8
  1. Jewelry making. I. Title.

TT212.C335 2010
739.27—dc22

2009031408

Technical Editor: Judith Durant
Copy Editor: Tamara Honaman
Book & Cover Design: Laura H. Couallier, Laura Herrmann Design
Illustrations: Julia S. Pretl
Photographs: All photographs by Glenn Scott unless otherwise noted.

Printed in China

Steampunk-Style Jewelry

VICTORIAN, FANTASY, AND MECHANICAL
NECKLACES, BRACELETS, AND EARRINGS

Jean Campbell

Creative Publishing
international

CONTENTS

6 Foreword by Paul Di Filippo

9 Introduction

10 Maker's Workshop

18 Basic Jewelry-Making Techniques

22 PROJECTS AND SIDES

22 Filigree Gears Necklace

26 Sidebar: Steampunk Roots

28 The Anachronist Necklace

32 Sidebar: Sci-Fi Origins

34 Captured Time Ring

38 Sidebar: Modding

40 Rubies in Time Bracelet

43 Sidebar: The Community

44 Love's Labour's Lost Ensemble

48 Sidebar: Topping It Off

50 Gearrings

53 Sidebar: About Lolita

54 Minerva's Folly Cuff

58 Sidebar: Dressing Up

60 Portal Explorers Necklace

64 Sidebar: Gear

aetheric scientist, given the urge and talent. Steampunks are makers and doers, not passive consumers and mere audience members—as this book well demonstrates!

The key allure and goal of Steampunk is to fashion and inhabit a world where the awe and romance inspired by humanity's pursuit of scientific knowledge is reflected in our tools, furniture, architecture, literature, art, and fashions. The mode is both a celebration of the past and of what might yet be, a witty commentary on things lost and paths not taken.

All of my foregoing philosophy is made manifest in the pages of this book much more vividly and emphatically than my mere words can convey. With a clear and informed and passionate vision of what Steampunk means, Jean Campbell has assembled a guild of talented jewelry makers who echo her goals and abilities. In lucid, revelatory chapters, they share the secrets of their hard-earned, joyous accomplishments, providing endless inspiration to lucky readers intent on entering the exciting world of Steampunk craftsmanship.

Cinch the straps of your aerostatic harness, dog the ports of your bathyscaphe, engage the drill bit of your subterranean burrower. You're in for a stimulating ride!

— Paul Di Filippo
author, *The Steampunk Trilogy*
Providence, Rhode Island

Introduction

"Steampunk...What's that?!"

That question is a common reaction from people new to the name of this style trend— one that's been around for more than twenty years, since the term was first coined in 1987. Generally, Steampunk is a fashion, design, and popular-culture phenomenon that combines romance and technology. Among its many influences are futurism, time travel, and the Victorian Age. These seemingly disparate facets combine into a resulting look that might be called "Mad Max Meets Jane Austen."

Signature Steampunk jewelry design pairs mechanically based found objects with Victorian-influenced filigree, charms, chain, and sumptuous beads to create one-of-a-kind pieces. Brass and copper are usually the metals of choice, and each piece often holds some kind of meaning —it tells a story, evokes a memory, eulogizes a historical figure or object, or simply evokes a hearty chortle. The look is romantic but not fussy; edgy but not angry; futuristic but not cold.

For *Steampunk-Style Jewelry* I've gathered together twenty pieces that embody the heart and soul of this trend. You don't need to be a master metalsmith to make these projects. A curiosity to learn, an explorer's spirit for shopping, and the willingness to pick up the occasional hand or small power tool are all you really need.

There's a design for just about any wardrobe. Show off your punk side with *Minerva's Folly Cuff* on page 54. Or firmly announce your (perhaps newfound) dedication to Steampunk by showing off the *Dirigible Aviatrix Necklace* on page 102 or the *Horological Faery Gadget Necklace* on page 90. Make a nod to Steam while wearing the *Voluminating Exhalator Bracelet* on page 108 or the *Tempus Fugit Pendant* on page 124.

The thirteen talented project designers featured in this book show you how to make their pieces through clear step-by-step instructions and illustrations. If you need to learn or relearn a specific technique to finish your project, you'll find them all described in the Maker's Workshop on page 10. Because many of the projects heavily utilize found objects, I've provided tips and resources on how and where to shop for them on page 144. There's plenty of inspiration in the sidebars showcasing the practitioners who have influenced and have been influenced by Steampunk. In the final section of the book, you'll find a gallery of Steampunk jewelry designs from some of this community's finest, hopefully to inspire you to do a little Steampunking of your own.

I hope you enjoy making the projects in this book and savor the truly innovative work of the artists featured throughout. May *Steampunk-Style Jewelry* serve as a steam-driven vessel for your imagination, bringing you to the uncharted ports and unknown harbors of your creativity.

Steampunk Ring
Daniel Proulx,
Catherinette Rings

Maker's
workshop

D.

The supplies and techniques you need to create Steampunk-style jewelry are pretty basic. Nearly all the pieces in this book are made with items you may already have on hand or can easily find on trips to your local bead shop, hardware store, or junk shop. A few hand tools are usually all you need to get the job done.

Materials

Beads (A) are my favorite part of any jewelry project. They are versatile, plentiful, and easy to find. In this book, beads serve as ornament to many of the designs. You'll find beads made of crystal, fire-polished glass, fresh-water pearl, porcelain, stone, metal, and vintage glass.

Chain (B) is a key component in Steampunk style jewelry. Its manufactured quality lends an instant Industrial Revolution vibe. Shop for both plain and fancy versions and make sure the links are wide enough to accept a jump ring or wrapped loop.

Eyelets (C) are two-part brass findings. They lend a smooth metal lining to a hole in metal or leather. Think lacing holes on a pair of Converse All Stars. Collage artists often use these for connecting papers and boards, so you can usually find them at scrapbooking stores. To set eyelets you need an eyelet setting tool, hammer, and block (see page 16).

A.

B.

C.

Fabric is used in some Steampunk jewelry. It contributes to the costume-y effect, but also adds a bit of softness and romance. *Minerva's Folly Cuff* (see page 54) employs stretchy *tulle,* a netted fabric you might see on a wedding dress or tutu.

Thread (D) is used to string beads and stitch fabric. I recommend a strong braided beading thread like 6-pound FireLine, especially when the thread comes into contact with metal.

Filigree (E) is historically an intricate type of metal jewelry design. Thin wires are soldered together to make curvy, interlocking shapes. The filigree in the projects in this book is stamped brass with delicate Art Nouveau-style designs. This type of filigree comes in a wide variety of shapes, from simple bars to butterflies. It can be found at most bead shops.

E.

FINDINGS are small, usually metal bits and pieces that connect your jewelry to form a whole. There are hundreds of types of findings. Here's a list of the ones you need to know about when making the projects in this book.

F.

G.

H.

I.

J.

K.

Bead caps (F) are cupped pieces of metal that fit neatly over the end of a bead.

Bezels (G) are flat metal disks with raised edges. They are most often used for setting cabochons, but also used for making resin-imbued collages.

Clasps (H) are the closures that connect the ends of a piece of jewelry to each other. *Hook-and-eye, lobster,* and *toggle* clasps are three of the most common types.

Connectors (I) link one part of a piece of jewelry together with another. They often have loops on both sides.

Crimp beads (J) are thin metal tubes used to connect flexible beading wire to another type of finding. You use crimping pliers to make the connection (see *Crimping,* page 19).

Crimp ends (K) are small loops of wire or a simple clasp with a crimp bead built right in.

Cuff blanks (L) are wrist-sized solid or mesh curves of metal that are used for embellishing.

Ear wires (N) are used for attaching an earring to a pierced ear. Two common types are *French ear wires,* which are U-shaped wires with a loop, and *leverback ear wires,* which have a snapping security closure.

Eye pins (O) are straight pieces of wire with a simple loop at one end.

Jump rings (P) are small circles of wire used to connect findings. Open them with two pairs of chain-nose pliers.

Split rings (Q) are doubled jump rings that are shaped like key rings. Open them easily with split-ring pliers.

Head pins (R) are straight pieces of wire with a flat metal disk or round at one end.

Lockets (S) are small metal case pendants that open and close with a hinged mechanism. They are meant for displaying photos or collages that can be concealed inside.

L.

S.

N.

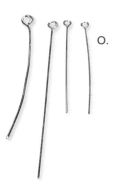

O.

R.

P & Q.

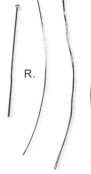

Ribbon end crimps (T) are flat solid strips of metal that are folded down the center lengthwise, with a loop at the center of the fold. They are used for finishing the ends of ribbon or leather to connect to a clasp or other finding. Because one edge has tiny teeth for grabbing, just use flat-nose pliers to squeeze this finding into place.

Rings (U) are large closed circles of metal, often decorative, which are used for embellishing jewelry.

Ring blanks (V) have a smooth face, which makes it easy to attach a ring top.

Found objects (W) are the flotsam and jetsam of everyday life and at the heart of Steampunk jewelry. What should you look for? Any fairly small object that evokes a nineteenth-century feel. Brass and copper are the metals of choice, and if the item you discover makes you think of mad science or time travel, that's a bonus. Here's a short list of things to look for: Watch parts, Skeleton keys, Machine parts, Monocles, Metal coat-check tags, Military medals, Monopoly-style game pieces, Tiny belt buckles, Vintage tins, Hinges and tiny latches, Badges, and Old lamp pulls.

W.

Shopping for Found Objects

When designing Steampunk jewelry, it's best to act like a raven, picking up shiny bright objects and bringing them home to your nest. Once you're in the habit, you'll find amazing things during walks along a beach, in back alleyways, and between the cushions of your couch. But there are more conventional places, too:

Online. There's a sea of found objects on websites like ebay.com and etsy.com. You order some materials (like watch parts and keys) by the lot. You'll get many of the items you're looking for, and a sprinkling of things you weren't expecting.

Junk shops, thrift stores, and **flea markets.** Although this type of shopping is subject to the whims of chance, it often produces the most unique results. Remember, what you're looking for is small, so explore thoroughly. Dig through bins, reach deep into cardboard boxes, and check out the bottom shelf of display cases. Sometimes the best thing is to interact with the owners—they'll be happy to point you in the right direction.

Surplus stores. There's usually at least one surplus shop in every big city, stocked with random leftovers from industrial manufacturers. You might not know what the flibberwidget that's caught your eye is called, or its purpose, but if it feels right, buy it! It probably won't be there on your next visit.

Hardware stores. You'd be surprised at the Steampunk items you can find the local hardware store. Visit the sections that sell little parts—like electrical, and plumbing supplies—and keep your eyes out for anything brass or copper.

X.

Y.

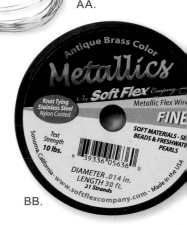

AA.

Glass cabochons (X) are solid glass domes with one flat side. *Floral gems* are the glass half-marbles you might see at the bottom of a vase or fish tank. You can purchase those at most craft stores. *Dew drops* have more crisp edges and evenly rounded domes.

Hardware (Y) is another key component when making Steampunk jewelry. Thin bolts and tiny nuts are perfect for that mechanized look. Lamp parts, electrical conduits, D rings, and drawer hardware are all easy to find at your hardware store and are great Steam components, too.

Leather and **faux-leather** give an Old World feel to Steampunk accessories. Work with recycled leather from old purses or boots or purchase pieces of scrap leather from a general craft store.

Milagros (Z), Spanish for "miracles," are small stamped metal charms that are traditional symbols of healing, popular in Mexico and South American countries. They come in a variety of shapes that generally depict the desired outcome of the devotion. Actually, any Victorian-era *charm* is good to add to your stash.

Printed paper offers lots of ways to evoke the special qualities of Steampunk. Cut-out vintage photos, book pages, postage stamps, and maps are just a few of the items that can be glued to findings, put behind glass cabochons, or framed inside lockets. All types of paper used in jewelry-making should be coated with acrylic sealer and allowed to dry before you glue it or apply resin.

Z.

Wire (AA) is a key element in just about every project in this book. Brass, steel, and copper are the most common types because their color and finish evoke that edgy machine-age look. Wire is measured by gauge; the higher the gauge number, the thinner the wire.

Flexible beading wire (BB) (brand names Soft Flex, Beadalon, and Accu-Flex) is a nylon-coated steel wire that is primarily used for stringing beads. Finish this type of wire with a crimp bead.

BB.

Watches and **watch parts (CC)** are integral to Steampunk style, tokens of time travel. *Mechanical watches* have beautifully intricate insides with delicate mechanisms that work great for embellishing jewelry; the more meaty bits of the watch works, with their built-in holes, are useful as links or in other applications. The insides of *quartz watches* aren't as intricate, but they're still fair game.

CC.

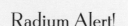

Radium Alert!

If your stash contains glow-in-the-dark watch faces or hands made in the early 1900s, they may contain radium, a radioactive chemical. As long as you don't put these items in your mouth and make sure to wash your hands thoroughly after working with them, the radiation risk to you is very low. I'd side with caution, though, and not use them at all—or at least certainly coat any radium-painted parts with glaze or resin.

 GG.

The short cure time means less chance of slippage. The regular version (brand name Colores) self-levels, so it's perfect for creating a glassy surface in a bezel or other cupped finding.

Ink (GG) is used for stamping on paper, glass, and metal. *Alcohol ink* (brand name Adirondack) is acid free, fast drying, and permanent on slick surfaces such as metal and glass. *Solvent-based ink* (brand name Stazon) works the same way—it just has a different chemical base. *Archival Ink,* made by Ranger, is a permanent dye-based ink that won't erode paper or photos.

Jeweler's adhesive cements (HH) dry clear. They are used to glue together nonporous items, such as metal. GS Hypo Cement, or watchmaker's glue, works well for lightweight items and has a fine-point applicator that allows for pinprick precision. E-6000 is a viscous, industrial-strength glue that is best for large or heavy items; apply it with a toothpick.

DD.

Acrylic sealer (DD) (brand name Mod Podge) is used for coating paper to seal in dyes. This sealer is also used to glue paper to another surface.

Dimensional adhesive glaze (EE) (brand name Diamond Glaze) is a water-based clear-drying coating that can be applied in a thin layer to create a lacquer finish or in a thick layer to create a raised glassy appearance. This glaze can also be used as glue to adhere lightweight items to nonporous materials. This product is water-based, so it isn't waterproof.

Epoxy resin (FF) is a synthetic polymer that dries clear, hard, and strong. You need to mix the two parts—the resin and a hardener—in exactly equal amounts for proper curing. The five-minute version (such as Devcon 5-Minute Epoxy) works well for bonding heavy nonporous items, such as found objects and stones, to findings.

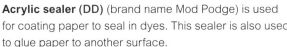

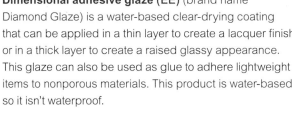

EE.

FF.

HH.

Texturizing medium (II) (brand name DecoArt) gives acrylic paint a sandy texture when the two are mixed. Use texturing medium to build up a surface, creating texture and depth.

II.

No Bubbles!

Bubbles are your enemy when working with dimensional adhesive glazes. There are several ways to reduce bubbles:

* Don't ever shake the glaze bottle.

* Turn the bottle upside down and let the bubbles rise away from the applicator tip before you squirt out the adhesive.

* Start the stream of glaze on a piece of scrap paper, allowing any bubbles in the tip to come out onto the paper, not onto your work in progress.

* Wave a match over the top of the glaze to make any bubbles rise.

* Use a pin to drag any bubbles to the edge of the piece, allowing them to pop.

Tools

At the heart of a Steampunk jeweler's studio is the workbench. Be sure to use ergonomically designed tools so the wear and tear of working with wire, found objects, and other metal items is a little easier on your hands, wrists, and elbows.

PLIERS grasp, turn, and bend metal wire and findings. They come in many styles, but you really just need a few to get started. Buy the jewelry-making type rather than the kind you might find at the hardware store, which often has serrated jaws that can mar metal.

Chain-nose pliers (A) have smooth, tapered, flat jaws with small tips. **Bent chain-nose pliers (B)** are similar, but have an angled tip for reaching into small places.

Flat-nose pliers (C) have smooth, tapered, flat jaws with broad tips.

Round-nose pliers (D) have smooth, tapered, round jaws with tiny tips.

Crimping pliers (E) have a rounded notch in the front of the jaws and a U-shaped notch at the back. They're used for squeezing crimp beads into neat, uniform shapes around flexible beading wire (see *Crimping,* page 19).

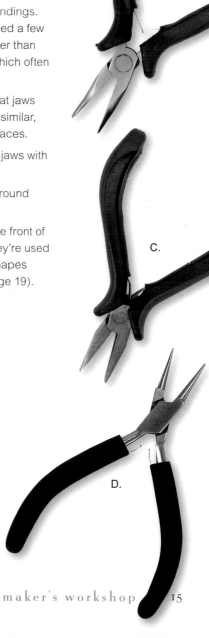

A.

B.

C.

D.

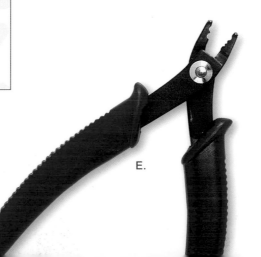

E.

Wire straighteners (F) are pliers with nylon-coated jaws. To use, squeeze the pliers around wire and simply pull the wire through. Repeat until your wire is straight.

Split-ring pliers (G) have pointy jaws with one curved tip. Wedge the curved tip between layers of a split ring so you can easily slide charms or other findings onto the ring.

Wire cutters (H) cut wire and other thin metals. There are two kinds of wire cutters you should have in your studio: heavy-duty and flush. Use *heavy-duty wire cutters,* found at hardware stores, to cut flexible beading wire and found objects. *Flush cutters,* found at jewelry-making supply shops or bead stores, are more precise. These cutters have a flat side and an angled side so that when you cut, one side of your wire is left flat, or flush. Use these for trimming thin wire, head pins, and eye pins.

Tin snips (I) are used for cutting tin and other sheet metals.

Heat guns are useful for manipulating the look of brass findings. This little machine produces a hot air stream, up to 1000°F (538°C). You can instead use the flame from your gas stove for this purpose, but the heat source is obviously not as precise.

High-speed rotary craft drills (J) are just about the only power tools recommend for beginner jewelers. Craft drills are very user-friendly, smaller than regular drills, and come with a variety of attachments for drilling, reaming, sanding, and buffing. You hold them like a fat pen.

Hammers (K) are important items in your workshop. A *jeweler's hammer* is usually made of steel and has a small flat face. It's used for flattening, texturizing, and work-hardening metal. A *rawhide hammer,* with a rawhide head, works well for flattening metal without leaving any marks. Hammer your pieces on a *steel block.*

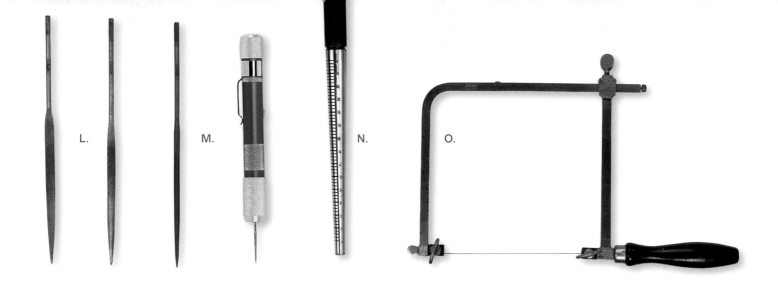

Metal needle files (L) help you file burrs and other rough edges on metal and wire. An emery board also works well.

Reamers (M) are straight diamond-tipped tools used for widening holes in beads and metal.

Ring mandrels (N) are tapered steel rods marked with ring sizes. Use them to bend and manipulate wire or other metals into a perfect ring shape. You can also use a finger-width wooden dowel for this job.

Jeweler's saws (O) have fine blades for hand-cutting items that are too thick to tackle with scissors or snips, but too thin to cut with a power saw. It's best to place the material you're cutting on a *bench pin* clamped to the edge of your work surface.

Sandpaper, steel wool, and **industrial nylon cleaning pads** (brand name Scotch-Brite) are good for sanding, texturizing, and aging materials like metals and glass.

Beading needles (P) are sharp, thin, and straight. They are so named because the needle's eye is the same width as its body, thus allowing it to easily pass through the small holes of beads.

Eyelet setters (Q) are straight tools with a flat point on one end. Place the front of the tool in the eyelet and hit the back with a hammer.

Scissors (R) serve a variety of purposes. Use one set of scissors for cutting paper. Use a second set for cutting fabric and thread.

Tweezers (S) are good for picking up and placing tiny items that are hard to handle, like watch parts.

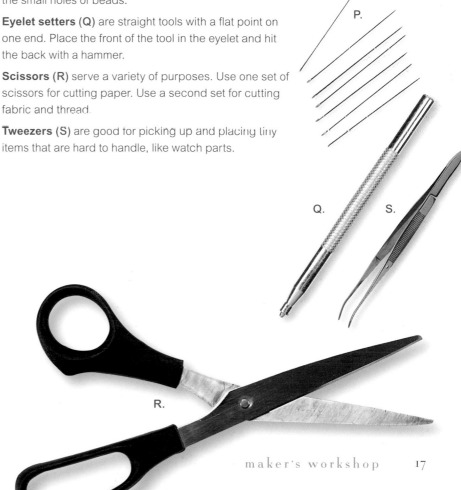

Basic Jewelry-Making
TECHNIQUES

Looks can be deceiving. Some of the jewelry pieces in this book may look like they were forged on an anvil, when, in truth, most were wired, strung, and glued together. The pieces are still extremely durable to wear, however. Another big plus is that the techniques you need to create these objects are very basic and easy to master.

Gluing

Gluing is about as basic a technique as you'll find, but I think it's worth noting a few tips. First, when adding glue, adhesive, or resin, work with a layer that is only as thick as the manufacturer recommends. This advice is especially important if you're working with adhesives and resin, because if you add too much, the outer layers of the product will dry solid and may even cloud over, often keeping the inside layers moist for a longer period than you might think.

Second tip: Never take short cuts when it comes to drying time. The glues and adhesives are often the backbone of these projects, so you don't want your piece falling apart because of your impatience!

Third tip: Use a toothpick or craft knife to remove any glue that's oozed out of place before it dries permanently —nothing screams "amateur" more than glops of glue on a finished piece of jewelry.

Finally, once you glue something down, check back on it every once in a while as it dries to ensure that the pieces haven't slipped out of position.

Opening/Closing Rings

There *is* a right way and wrong way to open jump rings. Doing it the right way ensures that the metal won't weaken, which would cause it to become brittle and snap.

Use two pairs of chain-nose pliers to hold the jump ring in front of you. Grasp the jump ring so one pair of pliers is on each side of the ring's split. Push one pair of pliers forward while holding the other steady. Close the ring by holding it in the same way, gently reversing the motion you used to open it.

Flush Cutting

When you cut wire with flush cutters, you'll leave one end of the wire pointed and the other end flat. You might need a magnifying glass to see the difference, but you can definitely feel the difference on your finger. To ensure that your wirework isn't pulling at clothing or scratching skin, always cut your wire so the flush side of the cutters is facing toward the work.

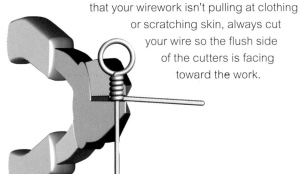

figure 1	figure 2	figure 3	figure 4

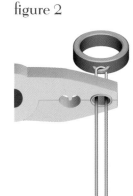 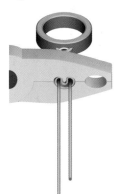 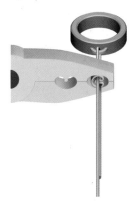

Crimping

Crimping is a technique for securing flexible beading wire to a finding. You'll need crimping pliers (page 15) and a crimp bead (page 11).

First, cut the amount of wire you require plus at least 2" (5.1 cm). String one crimp bead and the finding; pass back through the crimp bead leaving a 1" (2.5 cm) tail **(figure 1)**.

Pull the tail wire to snug the crimp bead to about ¹/₈" (3 mm) against the clasp. Grasp the crimp bead with the front notch of the pliers and squeeze. The round crimp bead will turn into an oval, allowing the wires inside the bead to separate **(figure 2)**.

Move the crimp bead to the back notch of the pliers and squeeze it into a U shape **(figure 3)**.

Turn the crimp bead 90° and nestle it into the front notch. Squeeze the bead into a cylinder shape **(figure 4)**.

Coiling

This technique, which consists of basically wrapping wire around another wire in tight revolutions, is another easy one that warrants at least one tip. The main thing to remember while coiling wire is to take your time. If you go very slowly, you can guide the wire with your fingers and pliers, making sure the wire will be seated in the right place. You can also instantly see whether or not you've wrapped the wire incorrectly. If you have wrapped it incorrectly, then you only need to unwind the offending wrap and start over.

figure 1

figure 2

Simple loop

Simple loops are made at the end of wires, head pins, and eye pins to form connections with other findings or wire. Once you've created a simple loop, you can open and close it just as you would a jump ring.

To make a simple loop, first use chain-nose pliers to make a 90° bend in the wire ³⁄₈" to ½" (1 to 1.3 cm) from the end (**figure 1**).

Use round-nose pliers to grasp the wire end. Holding firmly onto the body wire, slowly turn the pliers to form a loop. Continue turning until the end of the wire meets the body wire (**figure 2**). The resulting shape should look like a balloon on the end of a string, but not like the letter P.

Wrapped loop

This technique makes a permanently closed loop at the end of a wire. To begin, use chain-nose pliers to make a 90° bend in the wire 2" (5 cm) from the end (**figure 1**).

Use round-nose pliers to grasp the wire at the bend. Use your fingers to wrap the short end of the wire up and over the top of the pliers. Change the tool's jaw position so the bottom jaw is inside the loop. Swing the short wire end under the bottom jaw (**figure 2**).

Use your fingers or chain-nose pliers to grasp the short wire end. Wrap the end tightly down the neck of the wire to form at least two coils (**figure 3**).

Flush-cut excess wire close to the coils (**figure 4**).

figure 1

figure 2

figure 3

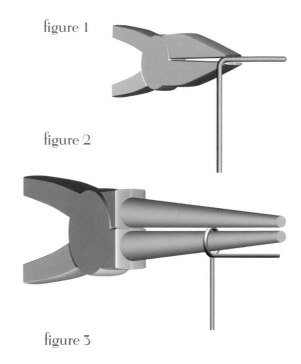

figure 4

figure 1

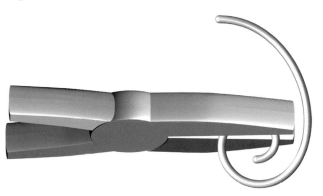

figure 2

Spiral

This technique produces a flat wire spiral. To make one, grasp one end of the wire with round-nose pliers and form a loop. Grasp the loop so it lays flat within chain-nose pliers **(figure 1)**.

Use your fingers to bend the wire alongside the loop. Adjust the position of the pliers and continue bending to spiral the coiled wire along the loop **(figure 2)**.

Hammering

Always use the right hammer for the job. For hardening, texturizing or flattening small pieces of metal, use a steel-faced *jeweler's hammer*. For flattening wide pieces of metal that might otherwise show hammer marks, use a *rawhide hammer*. Be sure to hammer on an appropriate surface, like a *steel block*. You don't need to get too enthusiastic while hammering jewelry-making components—a few simple taps will usually do the job.

Sawing

When sawing with a jeweler's saw and blade, make smooth strokes, keeping the blade as straight as possible along the cut line. Go gently. Most blades are delicate and can snap easily if you push too hard.

Drilling

To make holes for the type of projects in this book, it's best to use a small rotary craft drill (see page 16) and 1 mm to 2 mm drill bits. Be sure that you are wearing safety goggles as you drill and that you have an appropriate surface on which to drill, like a scrap piece of wood.

Filigree Gears
Necklace

DESIGNER: Cynthia Deis

Rivets, cleverly crafted from headpins, allow articulated metal lace disks to whirl around the neck. To intensify the vintage look, add patina to selected pieces of filigree with paint or with a heat gun.

Materials and tools

* 3mm black iris fire-polished glass beads (46)
* 30mm flat brass filigree disks (3)
* 38mm dapped copper filigree disks (3)
* 38mm dapped silver-plated filigree disk (1)
* 12mm dapped silver-plated filigree teardrops (4)
* 20mm dapped antiqued brass filigree teardrops (2)
* 8mm antique copper filigree bead caps (3)
* 1" (2.5 cm) brass headpins (9)
* 1" (2.5 cm) copper headpins (6)
* 18mm antiqued copper hook clasp (1)
* 10mm antiqued copper rectangular jump ring (1)
* 4 × 7mm antiqued brass peanut chain (12" [30.5 cm])
* brass-colored fine flexible beading wire (24" [61 cm])
* light green enamel spray paint
* clear enamel spray paint
* rubbing alcohol
* paper toweling
* newspaper or other large scrap paper
* heat gun
* flush cutters
* round-nose pliers
* chain-nose pliers

Creating Vintage Finishes

You can "age" new metal jewelry findings by heating the metal or by creating a patina on the surface with paint. These techniques will give your metal findings a time-traveled look that's perfect for Steampunk jewelry.

Heat: Use a heat gun, the flame from a gas stove, or a butane torch to darken a metal finish. Be sure to work in a well-ventilated area and to always hold the metal with kitchen tongs or cross-lock tweezers—it gets very hot! When the metal cools, you may choose to seal the new finish with a coat of clear spray paint.

Paint: Any clean metal surface can be treated with paint. Begin by thoroughly cleaning the metal with rubbing alcohol to remove any surface oils. A clean surface will hold the paint better.

Next, paint the cleaned metal with a brush and oil-based enamel paints or coat it with spray paint. Apply the paint in thin, even layers and allow it to dry between layers according to the paint manufacturer's specifications. Seal the finished piece with clear spray paint to create the most durable surface.

To achieve a vintage verdigris or "distressed" look, simply wipe the paint off before it dries. The paint will cling to the recessed areas of the metal. Start with clean metal and apply a single thin coat of paint. Wipe the surface with a soft cloth and allow the remaining paint to dry. Repeat with the same color to deepen the look or add a second color to enhance the antique appearance. Seal the finished piece with clear spray paint.

1. Use the rubbing alcohol and paper toweling to clean the filigree disks.

2. Following the instructions in the sidebar *Creating Vintage Finishes* at left, use the heat gun to treat one 30mm brass disk until the metal darkens. Set the disk aside.

3. Lay the remaining 30mm brass disks on a piece of newspaper. Working with proper ventilation, lightly coat the disks with green spray paint. Use a paper towel to wipe the surfaces, removing most of the paint but leaving some in the filigree's recesses. Let the paint dry.

4. Lightly coat the disks with clear spray paint to seal the green spray paint. Allow the disks to dry for at least one hour.

5. Cut the beading wire into two 12" (30.5cm) pieces.

6. Use one wire to pass through a 38mm copper disk from back to front, leaving a 2" (5.1cm) tail. Pick up one 3mm bead and pass back through the disk's filigree near the place you last exited **(figure 1)**. Repeat, working around the filigree circle to add a total of 20 beads. When you reach the starting point, tie the working and tail wires into a square knot and trim the wire close to the knot. Set aside. Repeat this step one time.

figure 1

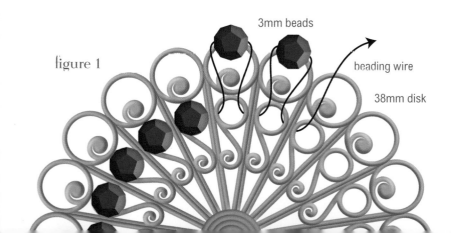

3mm beads

beading wire

38mm disk

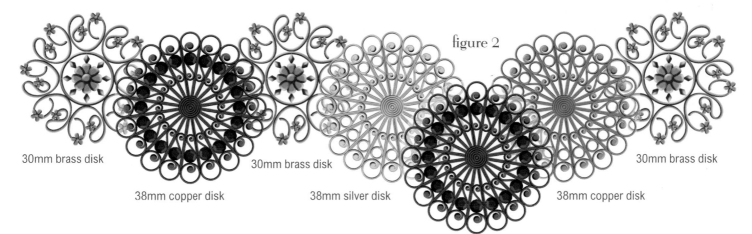

figure 2

30mm brass disk

30mm brass disk

30mm brass disk

38mm copper disk

38mm silver disk

38mm copper disk

38mm copper disk

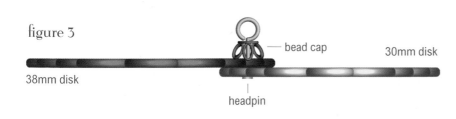

3mm bead

headpin

7. String one 3mm bead on a copper headpin. Flush-cut the wire ⅜" (9mm) from the top of the bead and use round-nose pliers to form a simple loop to secure the bead. Set aside. Repeat to make a total of six bead dangles.

8. Arrange the disks as shown **(figure 2)**. Pass one brass headpin through the left side of the rightmost 30mm disk from back to front and continue through the right side of the adjacent 38mm disk.

9. Trim the head pin to ⅜" (9mm) above the second disk and form a simple loop to securely attach the two disks. The disks should rotate easily. Attach the remaining disks in the same manner, paying attention to the way they are stacked.

Pass one brass headpin through the bottom of the center silver disk, from back to front. String one bead cap, trim the headpin to ⅜" (9mm) above the cap, and form a simple loop to securely attach the cap to the disk **(figure 3)**. Repeat to attach the remaining two bead caps to the bottom center of the second and fifth disks.

Use chain-nose pliers to gently open the bead cap loop just placed on the silver filigree. Attach one filigree teardrop and one bead dangle. Close the loop. Repeat this step to attach one filigree teardrop and one bead dangle to five more simple loops on the front of the necklace.

10. Cut the chain into two 6" (15.2cm) pieces. Use chain-nose pliers to open the end link of one chain and use the open link to attach the chain to one end of the necklace. Repeat to add the second chain to the other end of the necklace.

11. Use chain-nose pliers to attach the clasp to the open end of one chain and the rectangular jump ring to the end of the other chain.

figure 3

bead cap

30mm disk

38mm disk

headpin

Steampunk Roots

In 1987, K. W. Jeter, author of Morlock Night, coined the term "Steampunk" to describe a genre of fantasy and speculative fiction that later came to describe an entire artistic and cultural movement. Jeter and other modern fiction writers—such as Tim Powers, James Blaylock, William Gibson, and Bruce Sterling—influenced by nineteenth-century futuristic writers H.G. Wells, Jules Vernes and by Victorian-era technology and ideals, set their characters and action in Victorian and Edwardian times (circa 1850–1910).

Why? This period in Europe and America, which began with the Industrial Revolution and ended before the advent of the light bulb, was characterized by peace, prosperity, and an increase in the number of people in the educated middle class. Because both countries were enjoying relative prosperity at home, individuals had the luxury and freedom of thought to explore creative ideas. Innovation, invention, creativity, and a general sense of independence created a national buzz of excitement and energy. New mechanical wonders came to light as physical manifestations of human enterprise.

Victoria, Queen of Great Britain
and Ireland, Empress of India
(1819-1901). Photograph, circa 1895.

Photo: HIP/Art Resource, NY
Ann Ronan Picture Library, London, Great Britain

Steam road engines from *Trata do General de Mecanica,* 1895

Photo: Wikimedia.org

Influenced by the long-reigning British monarch, Queen Victoria, the era was also characterized by a rigid social order, social graces, and formal styles of dress—all of which provides modern writers with the perfect framework in which to hang Steampunk protagonists and villains that often challenge authority, society, and human nature.

Steampunk jewelry designs revel in this era's ideas and also in its gloriously elaborate fashions. Long coats, top hats, spats, bustles and frilly umbrellas were popular during this time, as were ornate metallic and jeweled pocket watches, rings, pendants, cameo brooches, and hair pieces. The elegance and intricacy of this finery is an excellent counterpoint to the hard-edged industrial and futuristic materials and forms that modern designers also incorporate to create pieces with signature Steampunk style.

Photo: From the author's collection

Marier Family, circa 1885.

FINISHED LENGTH: 24" (61 cm)

TECHNIQUES: opening/closing rings, gluing, wrapped loop, flush-cutting

The Anachronist NecKlace

DESIGNER: Margot Potter

This necklace design began with a charming Victorian photo portrait and quickly took on a cyborg vibe once it was adorned with an old watch widget. The designer and her friend made the Steampunk-style charms.

Materials and tools

* 10mm chrome jump rings (13)
* 23 × 32mm ceramic heart (1)
* 17 × 35mm pewter skeleton key (1)
* 25 × 50mm gunmetal key (1)
* 25mm metal watch wheel charm (1)
* 22mm gunmetal gear charm (1)
* 13 × 30mm gunmetal safety pin (1)
* 32mm round vintage photo (1)
* clear-drying craft glue
* 42mm gunmetal faux watch fob (1)
* 8 × 24mm watch part (1)
* 40 × 26mm gunmetal swallow (1)
* 15 × 20mm silver star milagro (1)
* 23mm silver heart milagro (1)
* 10 × 27mm silver hand milagro (1)
* 6mm silver jump rings (2)
* 27mm round metal watch face with holes at numbers (1)
* 25mm laser-cut wooden pendant with swirls (1)
* 26mm chipboard circle (1)

* 25mm wooden washer (1)
* chipboard number "6" cut-out (1)
* 11 × 36mm cork-topped glass bottle with hanging loop (1)
* assortment of 3mm–5mm watch parts
* 5 × 16mm question mark on chip-board (1)
* 2" (5.1 cm) silver head pins (4)
* 6 × 4mm white keishi pearls (3)
* 9 × 16mm crystal moon pendant (1)
* 32mm square acrylic tile (1)
* old book page
* 3mm smoked topaz bicones (2)
* 33 × 20mm pewter heart charm (1)
* 12 × 20mm brass hook clasp (1)
* 12 × 23mm gunmetal scroll link chain (23" [58.4 cm])
* 14mm chrome spring ring clasp (1)
* pitch black alcohol ink
* jet black archival ink

(continued on p. 30)

Materials and tools (cont.)

* metallic mixative silver alcohol ink
* extra fine glitter
* espresso alcohol ink
* burlap and vintage photo distress inks
* silver paint
* gloss luster clear acrylic sealer
* terra cotta texturizing medium
* black permanent marker
* chain-nose pliers (2)
* stamping felt
* applicator tool
* Bohemian flourish stamp
* hole punch
* harlequin background stamp
* foam square
* paint dabber
* Italian poetry background stamp
* high-speed craft drill with 1/16" (1.6mm) drill bit
* round-nose pliers
* wire cutters
* plastic comb

I. Open a 10mm jump ring and attach the ceramic heart pendant and the skeleton key. Close the ring. Set aside.

2. Open a 10mm jump ring and attach the gunmetal key. Close the ring. Set aside.

3. Open a 10mm jump ring and attach the wheel, gear, and pin. Close the ring. Set aside.

4. Cover the back of the photograph with a thin layer of glue and place it inside the fob. Glue the 8 × 24mm watch part to the left side of the face in the photo. Allow to dry. Close the fob and set aside.

5. Use the felt and applicator tool to apply layers of pitch black ink to the swallow charm. Allow to dry. Repeat to cover the milagros.

6. Attach one 10mm jump ring to the swallow charm and set aside. Use one 6mm jump ring to connect the three milagros and set aside.

7. Use jet black archival ink to stamp a flourish across the metal watch face. Use the felt and applicator tool to dab silver mixative in spots on the watch face. Use your fingertip to add a small amount of fine glitter to the silver mixative areas. Allow to dry. Add a 10mm jump ring to the top of the watch face. Set aside.

8. Use the felt and applicator tool to apply layers of the silver mixative and espresso inks to the surface of the laser-cut wooden charm. Allow to dry. Add a 10mm jump ring to the top of the charm. Set aside.

9. Punch a hole at the top of the chipboard circle. Use jet black archival ink to stamp the harlequin background on the front and back of the circle. Let dry.

10. Use the foam square to judiciously dab and layer the burlap and vintage photo distress inks over the harlequin stamp. Use the paint dabber to apply silver paint to the surface of the Italian poetry stamp.

11. Stamp onto the chipboard circle. Allow to dry. Cover the chipboard with acrylic sealer. Allow to dry. Add a 10mm jump ring to the top of the chipboard circle and set aside.

12. Use the drill to form a hole at the top of the washer. Ink the surface of the washer with vintage photo distress ink. Use your fingertip to apply small dabs of texturizing medium to the washer's surface. Allow to dry. Use the applicator tool to sparingly apply silver mixative to the washer's surface. Set aside. Use the felt and applicator tool to ink the surface of the number 6 cut-out with espresso and silver mixative alcohol inks. Allow to dry. Use a plastic comb to scratch the surface of the cut-out and re-ink with espresso alcohol ink to define the scratches. Glue the cut-out to the edge of the washer. Allow to dry. Add a 10mm jump ring to the washer's top hole. Set aside.

13. Fill the bottle with the tiny watch parts and the paper question mark. Seal the cork stopper in the opening of the bottle with glue. Allow to dry. While the glue is drying, apply silver mixative and espresso alcohol inks to the bottle's surface, leaving some areas clear and inking others to create look of old glass. Set aside.

14. String one pearl onto a head pin and form a wrapped loop to secure the pearl. Set aside. Repeat to create a total of three pearl dangles. Attach the crystal moon and the three pearl dangles to one 6mm jump ring. Use one 10mm jump ring to connect the beaded jump ring to the top of the bottle charm. Set aside.

15. Glue the book page to one side of the acrylic tile. Allow to dry. Trim any excess paper. Coat the back of the paper with acrylic sealer. Allow to dry. Use silver mixative and espresso alcohol inks to create the look of old glass on the tile's surface. Allow to dry. Use black permanent marker to draw a line along the tile's edge. Drill a hole in the top left corner of the tile. Add a 10mm jump ring to the hole and set aside.

16. String the following onto a headpin: one smoked topaz bicone, the winged pewter heart, and one smoked topaz bicone. Form a wrapped loop to secure the beads. Add a 10mm jump ring to the wrapped loop and set aside.

17. Use the brass clasp hook to attach the watch fob pendant to the center link of the chain.

18. Moving from the center toward the right, use the attached jump ring on each charm to connect to every other chain link in the following order: bottle, wooden washer, winged heart, milagros, watch face, and laser-cut wooden charm.

19. Moving from the center to the left, attach charms to every other chain link in this order: swallow, gears and pin, dream key, ceramic heart/skeleton key, acrylic tile, and chipboard circle.

20. Use one 10mm jump ring to connect the end chain link on the left to one half of the clasp. Repeat to attach the other half of the clasp to the other end of the chain.

Sci-Fi Origins

Photo: History Picks

The term "Steampunk" has been used during the last twenty years or so to describe a type of modern science fiction that harkens back to the works of the nineteenth-century writers Jules Verne (*Les Voyages Extraordinaires* series, 1863) and H. G. Wells (*The Time Machine,* 1895). The term was coined in 1987 by the modern science-fiction writer K. W. Jeter to describe a world that he and his friends had been exploring for some time—a world in which steam, not cyber-electricity, drove technology. Science fiction set in the time when steam engines ruled? That juxtaposition puts us squarely inside a mad scientist's work-shop in a glorious Victorian/Edwardian England during the days of the Industrial Revolution.

This style of retro-futuristic literature is, at its base, different than its cousin, cyberpunk. Whereas cyberpunk literature can be dark and brooding, often set in post-Armageddon landscapes, Steampunk is, at its heart, full of wonder. The world these characters inhabit is full of historical references. The Steampunk world is functional, logical, and very British, but full of untold adventure, risky experimentation, hidden dangers, fantastical monsters, outrageous inventions, and basic good-guy-versus-bad-guy scenarios. No matter what the storyline, whether horror or adventure, there is an element of filigreed romance in the pages of these books.

(top) Jules G. Vernes

The Steampunk Trilogy
by Paul Di Filippo, published in 1995.

Photo: Heritage Images

Les Voyages Extraordinaires
by Jules Vernes, published in 1863.

Although it didn't yet have its catchy name, this nineteenth-century style of science fiction started brewing again during the 1960s. Although their books aren't categorized as standing firmly within the Steampunk camp, writers like John Keith Laumer, who experimented with science fiction set in the Victorian era in his *Worlds of the Imperium* (1962), and Ronald Clark, who brought a high-tech doomsday bomb to a celebrity-filled nineteenth-century England in *Queen Victoria's Bomb* (1967), sowed the seeds for the genre.

Those seeds sprouted when Jeter wrote *Morlock Night* (1979), a novel tied into characters from Wells's *The Time Machine*. The prolific science-fiction writer Michael Moorcock (*Warlord of the Air*, [1971]; *The Dancers at the End of Time*, [1981]), set many of his books in Victorian England. William Gibson and Bruce Sterling wrote *The Difference Engine* (1990), the Steampunk novel that's credited for bringing the genre into the spotlight. The book features Charles Babbage's steam-driven analytical engine, which presses Victorian England into the computer age 100 years ahead of schedule.

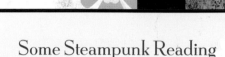

Some Steampunk Reading

Jeffrey E. Barlough: *Dark Sleeper* (1999); *The House in the High Wood* (2001); *Strange Cargo* (2002)

Stephen Baxter: *Anti-Ice* (1993); *The Time Ships* (1995)

James Blaylock: *The Digging Leviathan* (1984); *Homunculus* (1986); *Lord Kelvin's Machine* (1992)

Paul Di Filippo: *The Steampunk Trilogy* (1995)

William Gibson and Bruce Sterling: *The Difference Engine* (1990)

K. W. Jeter: *Morlock Night* (1979); *Infernal Devices* (1987)

Jay Lake: *Mainspring* (2007)

Ian R. Macleod: *The Light Ages* (2003)

China Miéville: *Perdido Street Station* (2000)

Michael Moorcock: *Warlord of the Air* (1971); *The Dancers at the End of Time* (1981)

Kim Newman: *Anno Dracula* (1992)

Tim Powers: *The Anubis Gates* (1983); *The Stress of Her Regard* (1989)

Philip Pullman: *The Golden Compass* (1995)

Lemony Snicket: *A Series of Unfortunate Events* (1999)

Captured Time Ring

designer: Barbe Saint John

Need an hour to last a little longer? Catch time in a web of wire and make it stop! This ring is a size 8, but you can adjust the number of wires, gauge, and wrapping to match your size.

Materials and tools

* 16-gauge annealed steel wire (19" [48.3 cm])
* 20-gauge annealed steel wire (5" [12.7 cm])
* low-tack painter's tape
* 26mm men's watch movement (1)
* wire cutters
* jeweler's needle files
* permanent marker
* round-nose pliers
* chain-nose pliers

* ring mandrel or finger-width dowel rod
* small jewelry hammer
* steel block
* rawhide hammer
* steel wool or industrial nylon cleaning pad

1. Cut three 6" (15.2 cm) pieces of 16-gauge steel wire. Straighten the wire with your fingers and file the ends smooth. Mark the center of each wire with a permanent marker.

2. Cut two ½" × 1½" (1.3 × 3.8 cm) pieces of painter's tape. Place them on the work surface with the sticky side up, about ¾" (1.9 cm) apart.

3. Gather together the 16-gauge wires and even the ends. Lay the wires horizontally across the middle of the tape pieces, placing the wires side by side **(figure 1)**. Fold over the ends of the tape to secure the wires, taking care that the wires stay flat and lie side by side.

4. Cut a 5" (12.7 cm) piece of 20-gauge steel wire and fold it in half. Place the folded wire onto the marked center of the bound 16-gauge wires **(figure 2)**.

5. Tightly wrap one end of the 20-gauge wire around the wire bundle seven times. Keep the 16-gauge wires flat and straight **(figure 3)**. Trim any excess wire and file smooth.

6. Repeat step 5, using the remaining wire to wrap the other side of the bundle. Use chain-nose pliers to flatten and tighten the wire binding.

7. Place the wire bundle on the ring mandrel at the desired size or on a finger-width-sized dowel rod. Use the wire-wrapped section as a center guide and use your fingers to gently fold the wires over the mandrel until they touch in the front.

8. Gently fan out the wires and interlace them **(figure 4)**. With the wires still on the mandrel or dowel, use a small hammer to gently tap the center of the interlaced wires, flattening them out.

figure 1

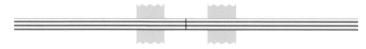

figure 2

figure 3

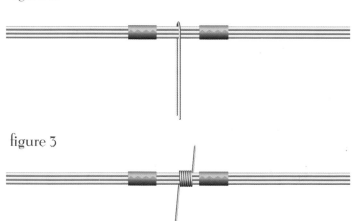

figure 4

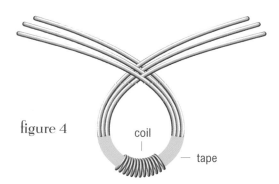

coil

tape

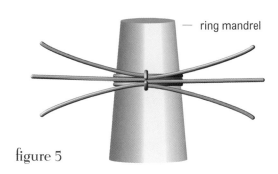

figure 5

ring mandrel

9. Cut a 1" (2.5 cm) piece of 16-gauge wire. Slide it under the center of the interlaced wires and fold over the ends to keep the interlaced wires in place. Trim any excess 16-gauge wire **(figure 5)**. Gently hammer the wire to flatten.

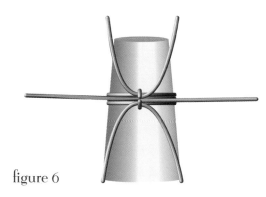

figure 6

10. Separate and fan out the 20-gauge wires until they are evenly spaced and look like the spokes of a wheel **(figure 6)**. Trim the wires so they each radiate from the center about 1" (2.5 cm). File and hammer the wire ends flat on a steel block.

11. Center the watch movement in the middle of the radiating wires. Use round-nose pliers to

carefully bend the wires into L shapes around the watch movement **(figure 7)**.

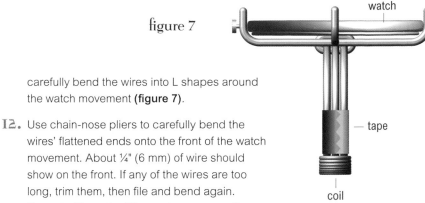

figure 7

watch

tape

coil

12. Use chain-nose pliers to carefully bend the wires' flattened ends onto the front of the watch movement. About ¼" (6 mm) of wire should show on the front. If any of the wires are too long, trim them, then file and bend again. Repeat with each of the spokes, proceeding with the spoke opposite the one you just bent in order to keep the watch movement centered.

13. Use the hammer to tap down the ends of each wire prong, making them flush with the watch movement. Use the rawhide hammer to gently shape the ring and the prongs if necessary.

14. Remove the ring from the mandrel. Remove the painter's tape and use steel wool or a cleaning pad to reveal some of the steel's color.

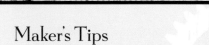

Maker's Tips

Steel wire is hard to manipulate and can be difficult to work with for a beginning wireworker. Make a practice ring in dead-soft craft wire first to get used to the pattern. A little practice will make it easier to work with the steel wire later.

This ring looks great done in copper, brass, or funky colored craft wire. Steel, brass, and copper wire are usually less expensive if you buy them at a hardware store rather than at a craft store.

Modding

Modifying high-tech objects, known as *modding,* is a key component in Steampunk culture. Designers challenge themselves to change an ordinary gadget, like a computer, appliance, or vehicle, so that it still works properly but resembles a contraption plucked from the pages of a Steampunk novel. Adding brass fittings, gears, fine leather, and lenses to, say, a cell phone, transforms it from twenty-first century ho-hum to Victorian Era huzzah. Makers who mod are hyper-inventive, always coming up with new ways to use found materials—often altering the items to make them more energy efficient, too.

Jake Von Slatt, proprietor of *The Steampunk Workshop,* is a tinkerer of the first order. He has retrofitted all kinds of familiar objects, including personal computers, guitars, cell phones, a car, and even a school bus. He frequently shares the step-by-step description of his work processes on his website

Photo: The Steampunk Workshop

Jake Von Slatt,
Victorian All-In-One PC.

Tom Sepe,
Whirlygig Emoto.

(http://steampunkworkshop.com) so that others can replicate his designs. Von Slatt emphasizes the recycled aspect of his work and considers what he does a political/environmental act or, in his words, "a sustainable rebellion." The photo at left shows one of his completely modded personal computers, complete with an old-time typewriter keyboard and a delightfully decorated monitor.

Tom Sepe is a Renaissance man fascinated with the Victorian era. He describes his *Whirlygig Emoto* as a "Steampunk-inspired hybrid-electric steam time machine that travels through time at exactly one second per second." He started with the frame of a 1967 scooter, tore out the engine and gas tank, and added an electric motor. The time machine wasn't complete, however, until Sepe added the propane-powered steam boiler to the back—it blows the whistle.

Rubies in Time
BRACELET

DESIGNER: Madelyn Smoak

FINISHED LENGTH: 7½" (19.1 cm)
TECHNIQUES: flush-cutting, simple loop, opening/closing rings

The tiny rubies imbedded in these upcycled pock-marked watch bodies glint like secret gems in this simple bracelet. The static vintage watch face reminds the wearer that there's no time like the present.

Materials and tools

* 25mm watch face (1)
* 5mm sterling silver split rings (2)
* 5 × 10mm sterling silver lobster clasp (1)
* 12 × 16 mm watch bodies (6)
* 20-gauge annealed steel, sterling, or craft wire (8" [20.3 cm])
* wire cutters
* jeweler's hammer
* high-speed rotary craft drill with #52 drill bit
* scrap wood
* metal file or emery board
* split-ring pliers
* bent chain-nose pliers
* round-nose pliers

Finding Watch Parts

You can find assorted watch parts at flea markets and junk shops, but etsy.com and ebay.com are also good sources. You might consider paying a little more for watch parts that have already been dismantled. This way, you can spend more time being creative and less time messing around taking things apart.

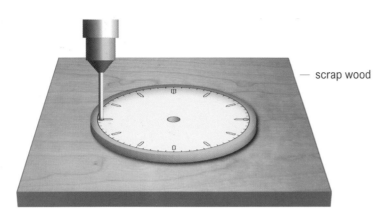

— scrap wood

figure 1

figure 2

figure 3

I. If necessary, use the wire cutters to trim off the wire spokes on the back of the watch face. If the cut isn't perfectly flush, lay the face, front side down, on the scrap wood and gently hammer the spokes to flatten them.

2. Lay the watch face, front side up, on the scrap wood. Determine how you'd like the watch to lie on your wrist. Drill holes at the 3 o'clock and 9 o'clock positions, 2mm from the edge **(figure 1)** Use a metal file or emery board to remove any burrs. Set aside.

3. Use split-ring pliers to open one split ring. Attach the clasp. Set aside.

4. Lay the watch bodies and watch face in a line, with the watch face in the center. Arrange the watch bodies so their textured sides are facing up.

5. Flush-cut the wire into eight 1" (2.5 cm) segments. Set aside.

6. Use round-nose pliers to make a slight bend at one end of a wire segment. Use bent-nose pliers to insert the wire into an existing hole on the right side of the first watch body. Grasp the wire tip while threading it through the watch body, then form a 4mm simple loop to encircle the watch body's edge. Over-turn the loop slightly to make a partial spiral **(figure 2)**.

Repeat step 6 at the other end of the wire, connecting the first watch body to the left side of the second one. Make this second loop in the opposite direction so the wire forms an S shape **(figure 3)**.

7. Repeat steps 6 and 7 to connect the right side of the second watch body to the left side of the third watch body, and the right side of the third to the hole on the left side of the watch face. Continue connecting all the components into a chain.

8. Repeat steps 6 and 7 to connect one split ring to each end of the bracelet.

The community

Seattle's *Steamcon* 2009 logo. *Designer:* Michael Montoure.

The phenomenon that started as an underground movement has coalesced into a full-blown subculture—Steampunk is an entire community unto its own. Steampunk followers frequent sites like *The Steampunk Workshop, Steampunk Lab, Brass Goggles, Steampunk Magazine, deviantart,* and *Etsy* to discover and discuss the latest art, fashion, and modding. Activists participate in online forums, share designs, and sometimes even post their how-to projects. Thousands of Steampunking craftspeople sell their wares on the Web, everything from goggles to garters, bracelets to bustles.

Steampunks do occasionally meet each other in person, however, through online-arranged "meet ups." During these short-notice planned gatherings, local enthusiasts dress in costume to attend events, collaborate on projects, and just have fun.

Steampunk enthusiasts also find each other at sci-fi, fantasy, and DIY conventions—some of which are entirely Steampunk-centric. In the United States, SteamCon, Dragon-Con, Maker Faire, and Burning Man are all popular places to meet Steampunks, enter costume contests and participate in "cosplay" (costume + play; see *Dressing Up,* page 58), listen to author lectures, collaborate in group artwork, and shop for Steampunk-style fashion and gizmos.

Steampunk Magazine, Artist: Claire Hummel
Steampunk Magazine is "a journal of fashion, music, misapplied technology and chaos. And fiction. It just may be the most spectacular magazine to ever fight against the spectacle, and it is free. Or as cheap as we can possibly get it to you."

Love's Labour's Lost
ENSEMBLE

DESIGNER: Margot Potter

Although named
for Shakespeare's
Elizabethan comedy, this
necklace is thoroughly
modern. The shape is
decidedly Victorian, but
gunmetal chains move
it from elegant to edgy.
Choose one pendant
or clip on all three for a
neo-Victorian mélange.

Materials and tools

* 1" (2.5 cm) sterling silver 24-gauge head pins (16)
* 8 × 10mm cream freshwater potato pearls (13)
* 3 × 5mm cream freshwater potato pearls (3)
* heavy flexible beading wire (6½" [16.5 cm])
* 4 × 7mm sterling silver crimp ends (2)
* 10 × 40mm onyx hexagonal oval beads (3)
* 5.5mm sterling jump rings (11)
* 16 × 32mm pewter bird on branch charm (1)
* 8 × 11mm silver-plated swivel lobster clasps (4)
* 11 × 36mm gun metal skeleton key charm (1)

* 22mm white/black ceramic square link with keyhole design (1)
* 23 × 30mm black ceramic heart pendant (1)
* gunmetal 5 × 13mm oval chain (22" [55.9 cm])
* gunmetal 6 × 8mm rounded diamond chain (11" [27.9 cm])
* gunmetal 8 × 10mm heavy oval chain (two 3-link sections)
* sterling silver ear wires (2)
* round-nose pliers
* chain-nose pliers (2 pairs)
* wire cutters
* large crimping pliers

figure 1

large pearl

Necklace

1. String one 8 × 10mm pearl onto a head pin and form a wrapped loop **(figure 1)**; set aside. Repeat to make a total of seven large pearl dangles.

2. Slide the end of the beading wire into one crimp end; crimp. Trim any excess wire inside the end's loop.

3. String {one onyx bead and three pearl dangles} two times, then string one more onyx bead. String one crimp end, then snug the beads and crimp. Trim any excess wire inside the end's loop **(figure 2)**. Set the strand aside.

figure 2

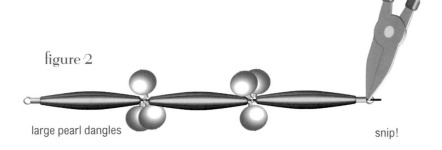

large pearl dangles   snip!

4. String one 3 × 5mm pearl onto a head pin and form a wrapped loop. Set aside. Repeat to make a total of three small pearl dangles.

5. Use one jump ring to connect the three small pearl dangles to the bird pendant.

6. Use one jump ring to connect the bird pendant to one swivel clasp **(figure 3)**. Set aside.

7. Use one jump ring to connect the skeleton key (through the center hole), one large pearl dangle, and the bottom of the key link **(figure 4)**.

figure 3

figure 4

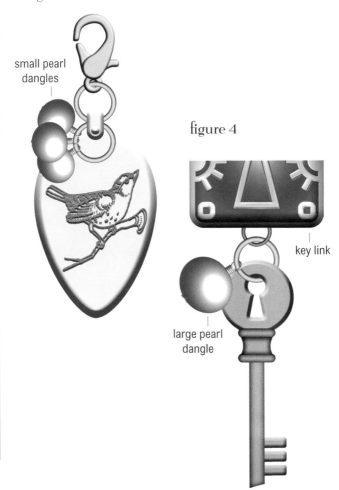

small pearl dangles

key link

large pearl dangle

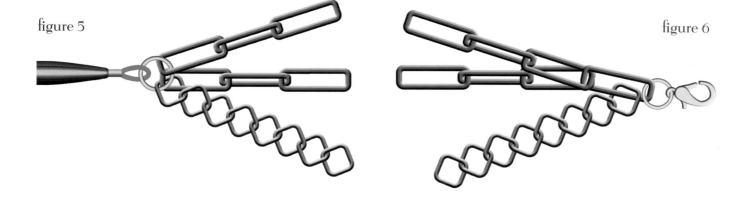

8. Use one jump ring to connect the top of the key link to one swivel clasp. Set aside.

9. Use one jump ring to connect the heart pendant to one swivel clasp. Set aside.

10. Use one jump ring to connect both ends of the 5 × 13mm chain and one end of the 6 × 8mm chain to a crimp end at one end of the onyx strand **(figure 5)**.

11. Fold the 5 × 13mm chain in half. Use one jump ring to connect the 5 × 13mm link at the halfway mark to one swivel clasp **(figure 6)**. Attach the open end of the 6 × 8mm chain to the halfway link of the 5 × 13mm chain.

12. Attach the key, heart, and bird charms to create the desired effect.

Earrings

1. String one 8 × 10mm pearl onto a head pin and form a wrapped loop; set aside. Repeat to make a total of six large pearl dangles.

2. Use one jump ring to attach three dangles to an end link of one of one of the 8 × 10mm chain lengths.

3. Use one jump ring to attach an ear wire to the other end of the same chain length.

4. Repeat steps 1–3 to make the second earring.

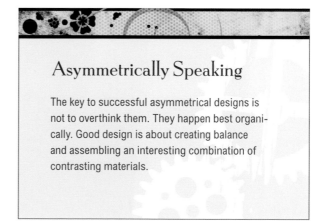

Asymmetrically Speaking

The key to successful asymmetrical designs is not to overthink them. They happen best organically. Good design is about creating balance and assembling an interesting combination of contrasting materials.

Topping It off

One of the most important features of a Steampunk costume is what's worn on the head. A top hat, leather flight helmet, curved bowler, straw boater, Arctic flap hat, pith helmet, Sherlock Holmes–style deerstalker, pirate's bandana, wool newsboy cap, or embellished tam. Each of these is the height of Victorian style. The list for Steampunk headwear doesn't end with what was stylish 150 years ago, however, nor is it relegated to only hats. Many Steampunk costume experts top themselves off with braids, feathers, tubing, wire, or yarn to add a bit of *Mad Max Beyond Thunderdome* punk style to the mix.

Kim Lee Dye, the brainchild behind Topsy Turvy Design, is a designer based in Oakland, California, who specializes in Renaissance, Victoriana, and Burlesque costuming and millinery. Her whimsical "hatties" are built from the ground up,

Photo: Silent Shudder Photography

Topsy Turvy Design. *The Beaux Top Hat.*
Model: Beaux Deadly

Photo: Maria Mann

Topsy Turvy Design. *Victorian Riding Hat.*
Model: Maria Mann

using buckram and wire that's trimmed with various materials. *The Beaux Top Hat* has a slight hourglass figure. It's covered with black velvet and embellished with double Swiss satin ribbon and nineteenth-century style millinery wings. Her velvet *Victorian Riding Hat* is adorned with saffron and metallic gold jacquard trim, burgundy coque feathers, and an antique cut-steel buckle.

Libby Bulloff, the artist and photographer behind Exoskeleton Cabaret, fashioned her amazing Steampunk *Headdress* from a set of black wool roving dreadlocks. She added strands of black split loom tubing and completed the thoroughly sci-fi look using silver knitting needles as hair sticks.

Photo: Libby Bulloff

Libby Bulloff. *Headress.*
Model: Jeana Jorgensen

gearrings

DESIGNER: Jen Hilton

These delicate-looking earrings are articulated in all the likely spots. As they gracefully dangle, they evoke a fanciful doodle found in the pages of a Victorian inventor's sketchbook.

Materials and tools

* 2" (5.1 cm) brass head pins (2)
* 16 × 22mm brass filigree connectors (2)
* 12mm pocket-watch gears with the pinions removed (so there are holes in the center) (2)
* 7mm wristwatch gears (2)
* clear jeweler's adhesive or resin
* 3mm light amethyst fire-polished glass beads
* 20-gauge brass wire (2" [5.1 cm])
* natural brass leverback ear wires (2)
* chain-nose pliers
* round-nose pliers
* wire cutters

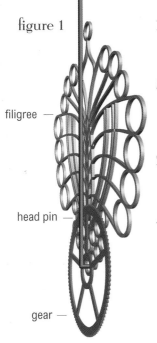

figure 1

filigree —

head pin —

gear —

1. Pass a head pin through the bottom hole of one connector (from front to back) and one 12mm pocket-watch gear (through the center hole).

2. Use chain-nose pliers and your fingers to bend the head pin at a 90° angle so it's flush with the back of the connector, holding the gear in place **(figure 1)**.

3. Use chain-nose pliers to form a 90° bend in the head pin toward the connector and even with the connector's top hole **(figure 2)**.

4. Pass the head pin through the top hole of the connector and use round-nose pliers to form a simple loop at the end of the head pin. Trim any excess wire **(figure 3)**.

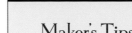

Maker's Tips

Depending on the type of watch you're working with, you can either unscrew the watch pinions or remove them with pliers.

ICE Resin is a good adhesive to use for this project because it dries crystal clear, offers an excellent bond, and may be applied with a fine paintbrush. Keep in mind that the drying time is a little longer than it is for other products.

figure 2

figure 3

5. Glue one 7mm wristwatch gear to the top of the connector, just below the top hole. Set aside.

6. Cut a 1" (2.5 cm) piece of 20-gauge wire. Form a simple loop at one end. String one 3mm bead.

7. Let the bead slide to the first loop and trim the wire to ¼" (6 mm) from the top of the bead. Form another simple loop to secure the bead **(figure 4)**.

figure 4

8. Use the beaded link made in steps 6–7 to attach the connector's top hole to an ear wire.

9. Repeat all steps to make the second earring.

About Lolita

*La Carmina
Mauve Coat*

Lolita is a Japanese fashion style that began in the Harajuku district in Tokyo in the 1980s. Because its base style is adapted from the styles of Victorian England, Lolita is considered Steampunk fashion's cousin. Unlike Steampunk fashion, however, which starts with nothing but a notion of neo-Victorianism, Lolita fashion starts with a basic anatomy that consists of girly and modest components, like a bow or hat, bell skirt, fine materials, and historical detailing. The wearer plays within that form, adding her own style stamp. Each "lolita" generally follows a certain subset within the style: Classic Lolita, Gothic Lolita, Aristicrat Lolita, and Punk Lolita are just a handful of the choices. Lolita is different than Steampunk fashion, too, in that the elaborate costumes are often purchased from commercial Lolita designers; thrift shops are often the source of Steampunk style.

The moniker "Lolita" is misleading for Westerners because the word brings to mind Vladimir Nabokov's famous novel of the same name. One might assume then that the style is a form of fetishism, but most likely the term's meaning was mangled in translation. Even though the book's namesake is a young, overtly sexual girl, the reasons for Lolita fashion are quite the opposite. Because the clothes are childlike, lolitas see the style as a solid rejection of revealing, sexy clothing. Lolitas would just rather stay cute, innocent, and carefree.

La Carmina Black Coat
La Carmina is a fashion designer, Japanophile, foodie, author, and blogger who specializes in Gothic Lolita. Her coat line features typical Lolita bell skirts with Gothic styling.

Minerva's Folly
CUFF

DESIGNER: Annie Singer

FINISHED LENGTH: 3" (7.6 cm) wide; cuff circumference is adjustable

TECHNIQUE: sewing

This mechanical cacophony of bolts, nuts, and beads is embellished with mid-nineteenth century style via a cancan-dancer-style tulle ruffle. It's an Old World cuff with a modern-day edge.

Materials and tools

* black nylon stretch tulle (1 yard [0.9 m])
* 2.5mm-wide silver mesh cuff bracelet form (1)
* 26mm brass mini bolts (18)
* 8 × 36mm silver banana clip machine parts, with a center hole large enough to fit over bolts (18)
* cog-shaped African brass trade beads, with holes large enough to fit over bolts (18)
* 4mm brass nuts (18)

* black nylon beading thread
* sharp fabric scissors
* reamer
* small bent-nose pliers
* sewing needle

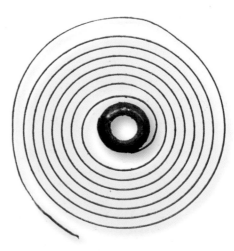

55

1. Cut the tulle into seventeen pieces, approximately 3" × 3½" (7.6 × 8.9 cm) each. Make the cuts so the stretch follows the long side. Set aside.

2. Use the reamer to slightly open the first center hole at one end of the mesh cuff. Open the hole just enough for a bolt to pass through.

3. Repeat to open a total of eighteen evenly spaced mesh holes down the center of the cuff (figure 1).

figure 1

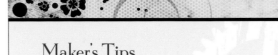

Maker's Tips

For a less spiky cuff, use shorter bolts or snip off the extra bolt length with a bolt cutter once the bolts are in place. You could also consider adding the bolts from the outside in and then clipping off the extra bolt length.

The banana clip machine parts in this bracelet are from a local surplus store, but any 36mm cylindrical machine part with a crosswise hole in the center will work.

Sewing down the tulle is a bit tedious, and you may stab yourself with your needle once or twice. The up side is that the blood won't be visible on the black tulle! Just keep at it. Sometimes you have to suffer to be beautiful.

4. Insert a bolt from the inside of the cuff to the outside through the first hole.

5. String on one machine part through one of the smaller holes, one African brass bead, and one nut (figure 2). Arrange the machine part so it's perpendicular to the cuff. Use your fingers and bent chain-nose pliers to tighten the nut.

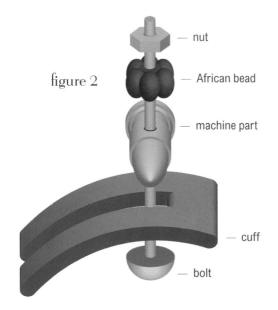

figure 2

— nut

— African bead

— machine part

— cuff

— bolt

figure 3

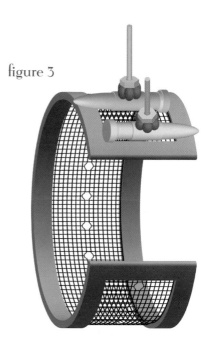

figure 4

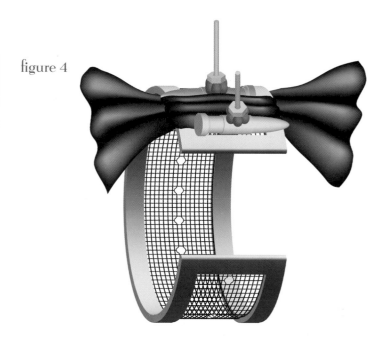

6. Repeat steps 4 and 5 for the next widened hole, this time facing the machine part in the opposite direction **(figure 3)**.

7. Tie a piece of tulle over the top of the cuff between the two machine pieces, joining it with a simple overhand knot on the inside of the cuff **(figure 4)**.

8. Repeat steps 4–7 until you reach the end of the cuff.

9. Pass 3' (0.9 m) of thread through the needle. Tie a knot at the end of the thread. Pass the needle through the fabric from the inside to the outside, at the edge of the cuff, catching all the layers of the tulle. Continue to stitch the tulle in place, working along both edges of the cuff **(figure 5)**. Stitching the tulle together will keep the knots from sliding loose and keep the ruffles in position.

10. Knot the thread and trim the ends.

figure 5

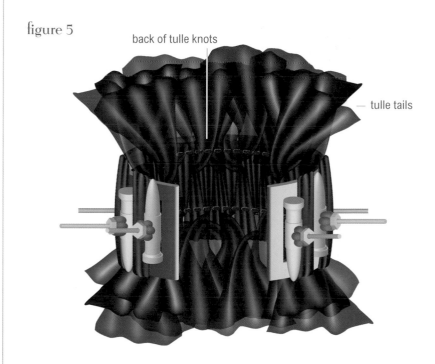

back of tulle knots

— tulle tails

Dressing Up

Themed costumes and dressing up are at the very heart of the Steampunk life. To come up with their one-of-a-kind creations, Steampunk artists turn to Victorian-era fashion to create their foundation and then build and embellish from there, adding Steampunk influences from fiction, film, and animation. The goal is to marry the sensibilities of Emily Bronte to the all-out rebellious attitude of a time-traveling Johnny Rotten.

Although some people are likely to wear Steampunk-influenced clothing every day, costumes are more over-the-top attire, often worn only at Steampunk, anime, or cosplay conventions. Costumes are designed and constructed specifically to evoke a character or vision from a retro-futuristic world.

Fashioning your own Steampunk-themed costume is a multilayered process:

1. Determine what kind of Steampunk you are. Genteel aristocrat? Wandering street urchin? Time-traveling sky pirate? Exotic belly dancer? Mad scientist? Other?

Libby Bulloff, of Exoskeleton Cabaret, is a master at styling Steampunk. Bulloff believes strongly in the DIY/noncommercial aspect of the Steampunk aesthetic, so she pulls together her ensembles from people's wardrobes and thrift-shop inventory. She then embellishes and accessorizes with handmade artisan objects.

Photo: Libby Bulloff,
Models: Francesco Longo and Rachel Westrum

2. Take inspiration from similar costumes described in literature or shown in film.

3. Gather nineteenth-century materials, like lace, tweed, cotton, leather. Consider how clothes were cut at the time—bustles and corsets for women and long straight coats for men. Also consider the subdued tones of the typical Victorian color palette. Look for Victorian patterns and textures, too.

4. Add a touch of 1970s-style punk style by adding industrial elements into your costume—maybe some rivets, brass buttons, chain, belts, straps, and other hardware.

5. Complete the outfit with at least one stand-out accessory. Top hats, goggles, parasol, spats, cane, wings, or ray gun are all good choices. And, as a finishing touch, don't forget to add a piece of the gorgeous Steampunk jewelry you've made!

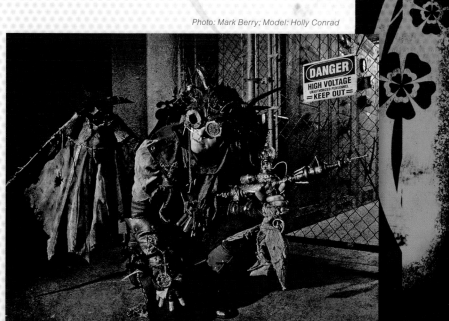

Holly Conrad, a.k.a. Fyriel, is an expert costume maker who's won numerous awards for her hand-made creations, including best of show in 2008 for her *Orpheus Alchemy Costume* (left) at *Steam Powered: The California Steampunk Convention*. This ensemble includes a set of mechanical wings that open to reveal hand-colored gauzy fabric and feather embellishments. This costume has what every Steampunk fairy requires—a backup steam-powered jet pack, leather-bound bottles, magical talismans and strands of beads, a pair of villain-focusing goggles, and of course, a pretty wicked ray gun.

Portal Explorers
necklace

designer: Jean Campbell

Pocahontas, Daniel Boone, Davey Crocket, and Jim Bowie—they all seem to peep out from time-machine portholes in this necklace made primarily from shiny brass lamp parts.

Materials and tools

* black permanent stamping ink
* 20mm glass blobs (5)
* white latex primer paint
* clear dimensional adhesive glaze
* clear jeweler's adhesive
* 29mm watch face (1)
* 1½" (3.8 cm) brass fasteners (5)
* ¾" (1.9 cm) coins or metal disks (5)
* 22mm brass check rings (2)
* 28mm brass check rings (2)
* 34mm brass check ring (1)
* 40mm brass check ring (1)
* 30mm brass check rings (2)
* 2" (5.1 cm) brass head pins (11)
* ½" (1.3 cm) silver conduit locknut; 28mm outside dimension (2)
* black beading thread
* gold size 11° seed beads (1 gram)
* 1½" (3.8 cm) brass eye pins (6)
* copper size 8° metal seed beads (13)

* 8mm brass melon beads (7)
* 5mm brass jump rings (3)
* 7 × 14 brass lobster clasps (3)
* 5 × 10mm shiny brass chain (12" [30.5 cm])
* 5 × 6mm antiqued brass heavy cable chain (12" [30.5 cm])
* 7 × 8mm antiqued brass long-and-short fancy chain (12" [30.5 cm])
* 7mm antiqued brass heavy rolo chain (12" [30.5 cm])
* explorers' portraits rubber stamps
* small paint brush
* tin snips
* hammer and block
* high-speed craft drill with 2mm bit
* wire cutters
* metal needle files
* chain-nose pliers
* round-nose pliers
* size 11 beading needle

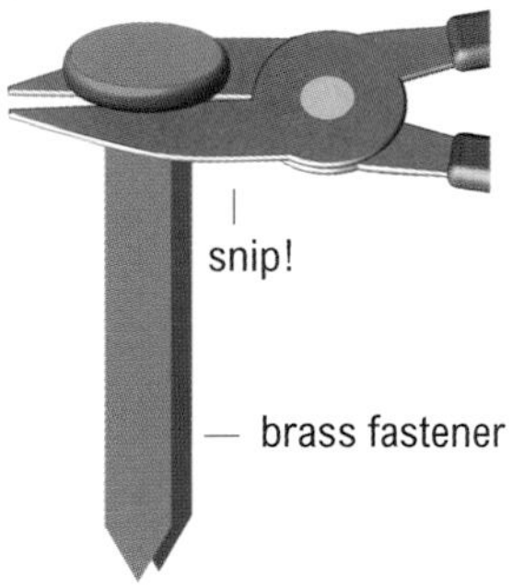

1. Working in a well-ventilated area, use the rubber stamps to stamp the back of each glass blob with ink. Allow the ink to dry.

2. Paint the back of the blobs with primer. Let dry.

3. Seal the back of the blobs with dimensional adhesive glaze. Set the decorated glass blobs aside to dry for at least twenty-four hours.

4. If necessary, trim the pins off the back of the watch face and file flush. Use jeweler's adhesive to glue one of the glass blobs made in step 1 to the center of the watch face's front. Set aside to thoroughly dry.

5. Use tin snips to cut the head off each of the fasteners **(figure 1)**. If necessary, use a hammer to lightly tap the head to tuck in any excess metal. Set aside.

6. Drill holes in the sides of the 40mm check ring at the 10 o'clock and 2 o'clock positions. Set aside. Drill holes in the sides of the 30mm and 22mm check rings at the 12 o'clock and 6 o'clock positions. Set aside.

7. Use jeweler's adhesive to glue a coin to the inside of a 22mm check ring. Glue a fastener head on the outside of the ring, covering the hole **(figure 2)**. Allow to dry.

8. Repeat step 6 for the remaining 22mm, 28mm, and 34mm check rings.

9. Pass one head pin through one of the holes drilled in step 6, from the inside of the check ring to the outside. Form a wrapped loop tight against the check ring **(figure 3)**. Repeat to add head pins to each hole of each check ring.

10. Use jeweler's adhesive to glue one glass blob to the inside of each 22mm check ring, making sure the top and bottom of the stamped image align with the top and bottom head pins. Glue one glass blob to the outside of each 30mm check ring. Glue the watch face to the outside of the 40mm check ring. Set all aside to dry.

11. Place a layer of adhesive inside the 30mm check ring. Set a 28mm check ring, coin side in, inside a 30mm check ring **(figure 4)**. Repeat for the other 30mm and 28mm check rings.

figure 1

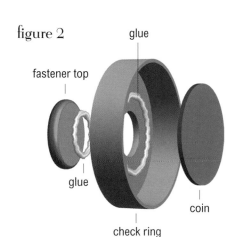

snip!

— brass fastener

figure 2

glue

fastener top

glue

coin

check ring

figure 3

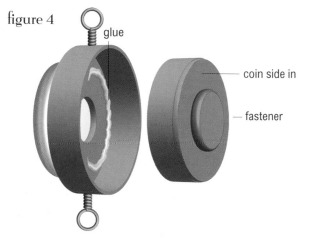

— head pin

figure 4

glue

coin side in

fastener

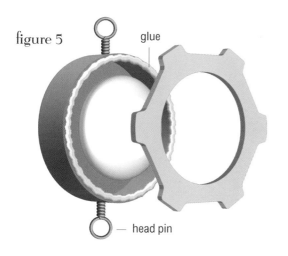

figure 5

glue

head pin

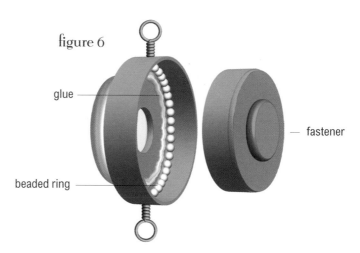

figure 6

glue

beaded ring

fastener

12. Add a layer of jeweler's adhesive to the edge of a 22mm check ring. Place a conduit locknut over the glue, framing the glass blob that's set inside the check ring **(figure 5)**. Repeat to add a conduit locknut to the remaining 22mm check ring.

13. Pass 12" (30.5 cm) of thread through the needle. String enough size 11° seed beads to fit around the inside lip of the 40mm check ring. Tie a knot to form a circle; pass through the beads again to reinforce.

14. Place a layer of jeweler's adhesive on the inside of the 40mm check ring. Tuck the seed bead ring inside the lip of the check ring. Place the 34mm check ring, coin side in, inside the 40mm check ring **(figure 6)**. Set aside to dry.

15. String the following onto an eye pin: one size 8° seed bead, one melon bead, and one size 8° seed bead. Form a simple loop to secure the beads and set aside. Repeat to make a total of six beaded links.

16. Cut the shiny brass chain into two 6" (15.2 cm) pieces. Use a beaded link to connect the top loop of one 22mm check ring to the second-to-last link of one of the shiny brass chains. Use a beaded link to connect the 22mm check ring's

bottom loop to the top loop of a 30mm check ring. Use a beaded link to connect the bottom loop of the 30mm check ring to one loop on the 40mm check ring.

17. Connect the remaining two check rings and second shiny brass chain to mirror the other side of the necklace.

18. String one size 8° seed bead and one melon bead onto a head pin. Form a wrapped loop that attaches to the end link of one of the shiny brass chains. Use a jump ring to attach a lobster clasp to the open end of the other shiny brass chain.

19. Open an end link of the long-and-short chain. Attach it to the end link of the rolo chain.

20. Repeat step 19 to attach the heavy cable chain to the same rolo chain link. Use one jump ring to attach one lobster clasp to the same rolo chain link. Repeat at the other end of the chains.

21. Attach the lobster clasp at one end of the gathered chains to the end link of the shiny brass chain nearest the beaded link. Repeat for the other end of the necklace.

GEAR

Great headwear (see page 48) and a pair of goggles (see page 128) are crucial to a good Steampunk ensemble, but rounding it out with some technical gear makes the wearer completely ready for back-to-the-future Steampunk action and adventure. Often working with found objects, artists fashion all manner of imagined accessories, including ray guns, radioactive material flasks, wrist-launching missiles, mini-dirigible hand pumps, time-travel-ready compasses, and weapons-ready convertible parasols.

These ray guns from New Zealand's world-renowned Weta Workshop were created by the wonderfully fanciful Greg Broadmore. They are just two featured in a series called *Dr. Grordbort's Infallible Aether Oscillators,* described as "a line of immensely dangerous, yet simple-to-operate wave oscillation weapons." Broadmore sells these "weapons" online, but the method of his weapons-dealing is much more involved than the usual sale. On the Weta website you'll find

Photo: Steve Unwin

Greg Broadmore, Weta Workshop.
Victorious Mongoose 1902
Concealable Ray Pistol.

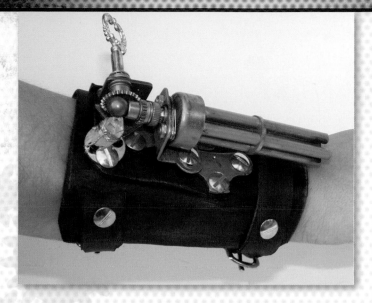

Aaron Ijams, Hexonal.
Wrist-Fired Gatling Gun.

detailed descriptions of the guns and their properties; "testimonials" (with accompanying portraits) of satisfied customers; and illustrations of the bestiary of the cosmos so you'll know what you're up against when traversing the planets.

Aaron Ijams of Hexonal created his *Wrist-Fired Gatling Gun* entirely with metal and leather construction. It's made from various brass findings and antique clock parts, and includes a quartz crystal nugget and copper wires to provide the aetheric "ammunition." There's a surprise—when you turn the key, the barrels rotate!

Greg Broadmore, Weta Workshop. *Lord Cockswain's Ray Blunderbuss "The Natural Selector."*

Photo: Steve Unwin

Time Traveler's NECKLACE

DESIGNER: Andrew Thornton

Slip on this necklace and fall through the portals of time. Unlock the secrets of the past and future with this mix of chain, natural brass, vintage finds, and fashion-forward design.

Materials and tools

* beeswax, melted
* clear jeweler's craft adhesive
* 20mm vintage metal watch face (1)
* assorted gold watch parts (5)
* 26mm fine pewter ring (1)
* 46 × 38mm brass filigree butterfly (1)
* 4 × 7mm brass knurled peanut chain (4" [10.2 cm])
* 4 × 10mm brass figure-eight hooks (2)
* 10mm brass jump rings (2)
* 14mm bronze bumpy ring (1)
* 1.5 × 2mm antiqued brass cable chain (3¾" [9.5 cm])
* 24-gauge gold-filled wire (23" [58.4 cm])
* 21 × 41mm vintage brass skeleton key
* 9 × 15mm copper faceted crystal horizontally drilled drop (1)
* 9 × 15mm smoky silver faceted crystal horizontally drilled drop (1)
* 6 × 4mm copper crystal rondelles (2)
* 8 × 36mm fine pewter tube (1)
* 8mm matte golden bronze vintage German glass bumpy round beads (6)
* 16mm sterling silver toggle clasp (1)
* 3.5 × 5mm brass chain (4" [10.2 cm])
* 2mm silver rolo chain (4" [10.2 cm])
* 7 × 12mm oxidized silver heavy cable chain (4" [10.2 cm])
* 5 × 6mm brass chain (4" [10.2 cm])
* 6 × 9mm silver flat chain (4" [10.2 cm])
* 2.5 × 5mm gunmetal flat chain (4" [10.2 cm])
* medium gold flexible beading wire (5" [12.7 cm])
* 2 × 2mm gold-filled crimp beads (4)
* 3 × 5mm pewter daisy spacers (7)
* 10mm pyrite chunk beads (6)
* wooden skewers (2)
* round-nose pliers
* chain-nose pliers
* wire cutters
* crimping pliers

figure 1

— 26 mm ring

watch face —

glue

1. Dip the end of a skewer in the melted beeswax. Continue until the end is covered, allowing the wax to harden.

2. Use the second skewer to dab the center of the watch face with adhesive. With the wax-covered skewer, place and arrange the watch cogs on the adhesive, keeping the edges of the watch face open. *Note:* The waxed skewer grips and easily moves the small metal pieces without sticking or getting your hands dirty.

3. Run a bead of adhesive along the edge of the watch face's front. Place the 26mm pewter ring on the glue **(figure 1)**. Set aside to dry.

4. Use round-nose pliers to fold the corners of the filigree butterfly around the pewter ring. Place the ring inside the filigree with the back of the watch face touching the wing tips. Use chain-nose pliers to squeeze and clamp the filigree edges around the ring, centering and securing as necessary **(figure 2)**.

5. Cut two 2" (5.1 cm) lengths of knurled peanut chain. Open the end link of one chain segment and attach it to the top left point of the filigree. Repeat to add the second chain segment to the top right point of the filigree.

6. Attach one figure-eight hook to the bottom left point of the filigree butterfly. Attach the other hook to the bottom right point **(figure 3)**.

7. Connect one jump ring to each of the hooks placed in the previous step. Before closing the rings, add the bronze ring **(figure 4)**. Set aside.

8. Cut one 2" (5.1 cm), one 1" (2.5 cm), and one ¾" (1.9 cm) lengths of 1.5 × 2mm brass chain. Set aside.

9. Cut 3" (7.6 cm) of 24-gauge wire. Wrap the center of the wire around the key three times. End with both wire ends pointing up **(figure 5)**.

10. Wrap one wire end around the other three times, coiling close to the key **(figure 6)**; trim the wrapping wire close to the wrap.

11. Use the remaining wire end to form a wrapped loop that attaches to one end of the 2" (5.1 cm) length of 1.5 × 2mm brass chain. Make enough wraps to meet the first coils made in this step **(figure 7)**. Trim the excess wire and use chain-nose pliers to tuck in the tails.

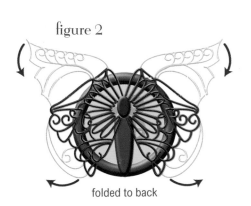

figure 2

folded to back

figure 3

figure 4

figure 5

figure 6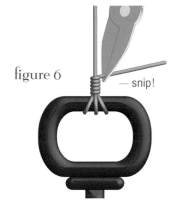
— snip!

figure 7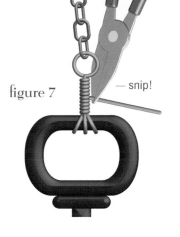
— snip!

figure 8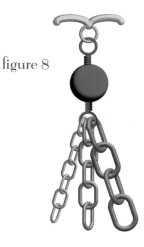

12. Cut 3" (7.6 cm) of 24-gauge wire. Pass the wire through the copper crystal drop and bend the ends up to make a U shape.

13. Form a wrapped-loop bail as you did with the key, this time attaching to the end of the 1" (2.5 cm) 1.5 × 2mm brass chain. Repeat with the smoky silver crystal drop and the ¾" (1.9 cm) 1.5 × 2mm brass chain.

14. Cut 2½" (6.4 cm) of 24-gauge wire. Form a wrapped loop at one end that connects to the bronze ring. Form another wrapped loop that connects to the open end links of the three lengths of 1.5 × 2mm brass chain.

15. Cut 3½" (8.9 cm) of 24-gauge wire. Form a wrapped loop at one end that attaches to the end link of the peanut chain connected to the right side of the filigree. String the following onto the wire: one crystal rondelle, one pewter tube, and one crystal rondelle. Form another wrapped loop to secure the beads.

16. Cut 2" (5.1 cm) of 24-gauge wire. Form a wrapped loop that attaches to the last loop made in step 15. String one vintage glass round. Form a wrapped loop that attaches to the ring half of the toggle clasp.

17. Cut 2" (5.1 cm) of 24-gauge wire. Form a wrapped loop that attaches to the bar side of the toggle clasp. String one vintage glass round

bead. Form a wrapped loop that attaches to all three end links of the 3.5 × 5mm antiqued brass chain, the 2mm silver rolo chain, and the 7 × 12mm oxidized silver heavy cable chain (**figure 8**).

18. Cut 5" (12.7 cm) of 24-gauge wire. Form a wrapped loop that attaches to the other end links of the three chains. String three vintage glass round beads. Form a wrapped loop that attaches to all three end links of the 5 × 6mm brass chain, the 6 × 9mm silver flat chain, and the 2.5 × 5mm gunmetal flat chain.

19. Cut 2" (5.1 cm) of 24-gauge wire. Form a wrapped loop that attaches to the other end links of the chains placed in step 18. String one vintage glass round bead. Form a wrapped loop to secure the bead.

20. String two crimp beads onto the beading wire. Pass the wire through the last loop made in step 19 and back through the crimp beads, leaving a ¾" (1.9 cm) tail. Crimp tubes. String {one spacer and one pyrite chunk bead} six times. String one spacer and two crimp beads. Pass through the end link of the peanut chain attached to the left side of the butterfly and back through the crimp beads (**figure 9**). Snug the beads and crimp; trim any excess wire.

figure 9

2-D STEAMPUNK

Steampunk fiction's fanciful imagery is rich fodder for illustrators working to convey an idea through an image. An artist working in two dimensions can capitalize on the many concepts and metaphors within the genre (for example, man vs. machine, technology gone out of control, the dangers of over-industrialization). Mechanical contraptions might portray industry, corporations, or automated processes. Seemingly old-fashioned Victorian characters caught in the midst of burgeoning technology might express the perils of progress, confusion, or fear. Mad scientists might convey creativity, innovation, or horror.

Award-winning illustrator and animator Richard Borge often uses elements of Steampunk in his mixed-media artwork. In *censorship*, a mechanical eye is trapped within a cage, and a mannequin guardian controls the only key. In *legislation*, Borge uses Steampunk-style gears, wires, cogs, and rivets to create a Rube Goldberg–like contraption. In *transhuman*, a retro-futuristic helmet (complete with propeller) and the side sketches suggest a mastermind at work.

Photo: Richard Borge

Richard Borge.
censorship, mixed media.

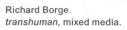

Richard Borge.
transhuman, mixed media.

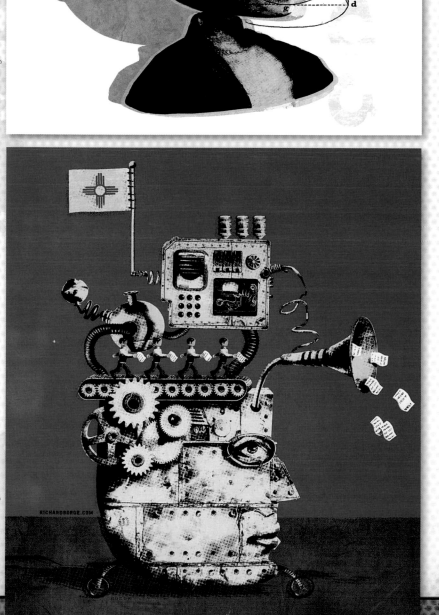

Richard Borge.
legislation, mixed media.

White Star Line
NecKLace

DESIGNER: Jane Mormino

The scrubbed-mirror charms that grace this haunting necklace are like souvenirs captured mid-sink from the *Titanic*, the *Atlantic*, or another of the ill-fated ocean steamliners in the famous White Star Line.

Materials and tools

* 18mm round glass mirrors (2)
* 35mm round glass mirror (1)
* selection of 20–35mm steamliner-themed postage stamps (4)
* 12 × 16mm brass two-hole oval link (1)
* 27mm brass eyelet cabochon settings (3)
* dictionary text or other decorative paper
* 26 × 15mm pewter steam liner game piece
* 5 × 6mm brass heavy cable chain (13" [33 cm])
* 15mm brass filigree square (2)
* 7mm brass spring ring clasp (1)
* 5 × 6mm brass extender chain (1¾" [4.5 cm])
* 2" (5.1 cm) brass head pins (4)
* 3mm watch gears or bead caps (4)

* cream 4mm crystal pearls (14)
* 2" (5.1 cm) brass eye pins (3)
* 3 × 4mm brass oval jump rings (3)
* clear dimensional adhesive glaze
* two-part clear epoxy resin
* 150-grit sandpaper
* cotton cloth
* small paint brush
* jeweler's adhesive cement
* pencil
* scissors
* small plastic cup
* plastic stir stick
* chain-nose pliers
* round-nose pliers
* flush cutters
* craft knife with sharp blade and appropriate cutting surface

1. Use the sandpaper to gently sand the back of each mirror, concentrating on the center of each. Leave a bit of the mirror glaze around the edges for a distressed look. Wipe away any dust with a damp, clean cloth.

2. Use the small brush to paint the back of one mirror with dimensional adhesive glaze.

3. Center one of the stamps on the mirror, face into the glaze. Press the stamp gently outward from the center to remove any bubbles/creases. Repeat for the other mirrors. Allow to dry overnight.

4. Add a small amount of jeweler's cement to the top center back of the 35mm mirror. Place the brass oval link on the cement face down so that one hole sticks out from the edge of the mirror (**figure 1**).

5. Trace one of the 18mm mirrors on the remaining stamp. Cut out the circle. Use a small amount of dimensional adhesive glaze to glue the stamp into a cabochon setting, being careful not to get any glaze on the front of the stamp. Allow to dry.

6. Use a small amount of jeweler's cement to glue the game piece onto the front of the cabochon setting from step 5. Allow to dry one hour.

7. Follow the manufacturer's directions to mix a small amount of two-part resin in the plastic cup. Very carefully, pour the resin into the cabochon setting. Fill the cup of the setting, being careful not to let it overflow or get on the front of the game piece (**figure 2**). The resin will secure the game piece into place permanently. Allow to dry for twenty-four hours.

8. Use a small amount of jeweler's cement to glue one 18mm mirror to the center of a cabochon setting. Make sure the image is right side up. Set aside to dry. Repeat for other mirror.

9. Use dimensional adhesive glaze to glue decorative or dictionary text paper over the back of the 35mm mirror, covering the back of the stamp. You can choose to add other glazed images on the back, too. Use the craft knife to trim the edges as necessary. Use the small brush to paint an even coat of glaze over the entire back. Allow to dry for four to six hours.

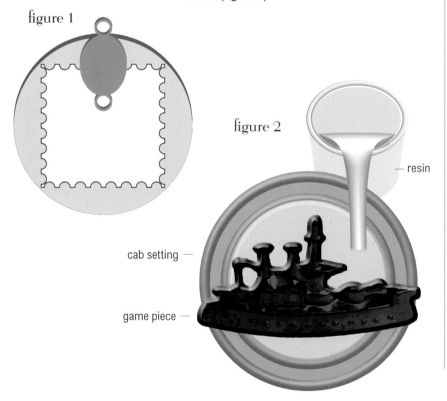

figure 1

figure 2

resin

cab setting

game piece

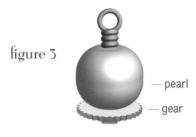

figure 3

— pearl
— gear

figure 4

figure 5

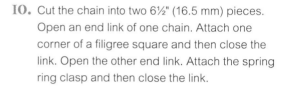

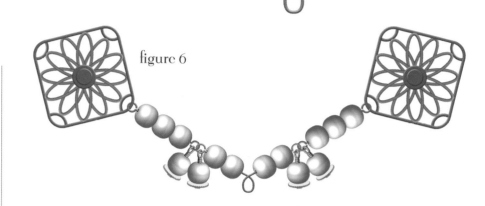

figure 6

10. Cut the chain into two 6½" (16.5 mm) pieces. Open an end link of one chain. Attach one corner of a filigree square and then close the link. Open the other end link. Attach the spring ring clasp and then close the link.

11. Open an end link of the remaining chain and attach one corner of the other filigree square. Close the link. Open the other end link and attach the extender chain. Close the link.

12. String one watch gear and one pearl onto a head pin. Form a wrapped loop and set aside **(figure 3)**. Repeat to make a total of four pearl dangles.

13. String three pearls onto an eye pin and let the pearls slide to the eye. Trim the straight wire to ¼" (6 mm) from the last pearl. Form a simple loop to secure the pearls **(figure 4)**. Set aside. Repeat to make another pearl link.

14. String two pearls. Use round-nose pliers to form a loop close to the second pearl. String two more pearls and form a simple loop to secure the beads. The resulting shape should look like a wide V **(figure 5)**.

15. Connect one beaded link from step 12 to the opposite corner from the chain connected to one filigree square. Connect the beaded V link

from step 13 to the beaded link just placed, adding a pearl dangle to each loop before closing. Use the remaining beaded link from step 12 to connect the open end of the V link, just placed, to the opposite corner from the chain connected to the second filigree square. Add one pearl dangle to each loop of the link-to-V connection **(figure 6)**.

16. Use a jump ring to attach the 35mm mirror pendant to the loop at the center of the V shape.

17. Use a jump ring to attach one 18mm mirrored cabochon to the bottom of a filigree square. Repeat to add the second 18mm cabochon to the second square.

18. Use a jump ring to connect the game piece cabochon to the end of the extender chain.

Steampunk
sound

Steampunk as a musical style can be hard to pin down. There are definite gothic, industrial, synth-pop, dark wave, and new wave overtones, but there are also hints of orchestral, ragtime, cabaret, Indian, gypsy, and even traditional klezmer music. As a whole Steampunk-style music is best described as eclectic, just the sort of mix you might get from a gramophone-toting time-traveling DJ from the nineteenth century.

Much of what brands this type of music as "Steam-punk" are the stage shows. Instruments, speakers, amps, and microphones are often transformed into what look like gizmos from a Victorian-era secret laboratory, with strobes, chains, knobs, and gears. The band members wear period costumes, often sporting unusual accessories that make them appear as though they've just stepped out of a souped-up Zeppelin or shiny brass time machine. The parade of belly dancers, pirates, acrobats, fire-breathers, ballerinas, and whirling dervishes contributes to what Steampunk band *Abney Park* calls,

Photo: Libby Bulloff

Abney Park is a Seattle-based band that was one of the first to take on the Steampunk tag to describe their unique musical style. Their musical performances are theatrical, visual, and filled with industrial beat and world-music overtones. The five band members (Nathaniel Johnstone, Robert Brown, Finn Von Claret, Kristina Erickson, and Daniel C.) portray themselves as pirates on the airship HMS *Ophelia,* ready to set off for adventures in an "era that never was, but one that we wish had been."

Photo: Jim Ferreira

Photo: Darren "Penance" Spinelli

Unextraordinary Gentlemen was conceived in 2006 by Los Angeleno Richard Pilawski to create a sound for Victorian fantasy fiction. Pilawski's drum machine, bass, and keyboards are teamed with Jennifer Pomerantz's violin, Eric Schreek's vocals, and "The Indifference Machine," a laptop within an art installation that Pilawski calls a "cross between a gramophone and an orchestrion." The resulting sound is both industrial and synth-punk, beautifully making audible the ideas in a Wellsian epic.

when describing its shows, as a "post-apocalyptic, swashbuckling, Steampunk musical mayhem."

Another key element in Steampunk music is experimentation. Listeners will certainly hear a rock band-type troika (guitar, drums, keyboard), but Steampunk bands usually offer an eclectic array of other instruments, too. Balalaikas, violins, accordions, harmonicas, trombones, cellos, and even bagpipes are all likely to be found in a time-traveling troubadour's bag of tricks.

To sample Steampunk style music, an Internet search will do, but *The Clockwork Cabaret,* a weekly radio show from Chapel Hill, North Carolina, will save you the searching. According to its website (www.clockworkcabaret.com), the show features "Music o' Gears, an anachronistic style of music that will make you long for the days gone by." It features "Sky Pirate Radio," regaling audiences with tales of adventures aboard the airship *Calpurnia*.

Vernian Process is the San Franciscan duo Joshua A. Pfeiffer and Martin Irigoyen. This musical collective began "with the sole intention of creating music that could accompany Steampunk adventures in one's own mind." The music flows like a movie score, ranging from hard-edged Industrial rhythms to gentle arias that are suitable listening while soaring on a dirigible.

A Few Steampunk Bands

Abney Park

The Cassettes

China Steamengine

Clockwork Dolls

Dresden Dolls

Ghostfire

Gogol Bordello

Ego Likeness

Faun Fables

Platform One

Rasputina

Sleepytime Gorilla Museum

The Stand

Unextraordinary Gentlemen

Vernian Process

Voltaire

FINISHED LENGTH: 18" (45.7 cm)

TECHNIQUES: wrapped loop, flush-cutting, opening/closing rings

Steam Voyageur
Necklace

DESIGNER: Jean Yates

This necklace features a handmade fine silver focal piece reminiscent of a Native American canoe. The canoe "floats" on a river of chains and hardware, to the gentle jangle and sway of Steampunk-style porcelain charms.

Materials and tools

* 20-gauge brass wire (56" [1.4 m])
* 4 × 14mm bronze bullet beads (14)
* 5mm gunmetal jump rings (54)
* 3mm African brass heishi (40)
* 18-gauge sterling silver dead-soft round wire (8" [20.3 cm])
* 15 × 7mm green porcelain screw bead (1)
* 15 × 7mm iron porcelain gear bead (1)
* 20 × 53 × 12mm fine silver pod pendant (1)
* 15 × 7mm rusty porcelain zig wheel bead (1)
* 15 × 7mm oxidized porcelain pinion screw bead (1)
* 7 × 14 gunmetal lobster clasps (16)
* 20mm oxidized porcelain round steam gear link (2)
* 3mm 18-gauge gunmetal rolo chain (23" [58.4 cm])

* 22mm moss porcelain square compass charm (1)
* 6 × 25mm rusty porcelain screw link (1)
* 2" (5.1cm) bronze 20-gauge head pins (6)
* 4 × 5mm fuchsia fire-polished glass rondelles (2)
* 22mm rusty porcelain square porthole link (1)
* 6 × 25mm pine porcelain screw link (1)
* 22mm green porcelain timepiece link (1)
* 20mm fine silver toggle clasp (1)
* 12mm pine porcelain square bolt bead (1)
* 12mm green porcelain round bolt bead (1)
* 22mm motor oil porcelain square keyhole charm (1)

(continued on p. 80)

figure 1

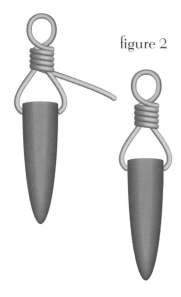

figure 2

Materials and tools (cont.)

* 6 × 25mm iron porcelain screw link (1)
* 4 × 5mm teal fire-polished glass rondelles (2)
* 22mm oxidized porcelain square keyhole link (1)
* 6 × 25mm moss porcelain screw link (1)
* 20mm rust porcelain square belt buckle link (1)
* 15mm oxidized porcelain round steam gear charm (1)
* 6 × 25mm green porcelain screw charm (1)
* wire cutters
* chain-nose pliers (2 pairs)
* round-nose pliers

figure 3

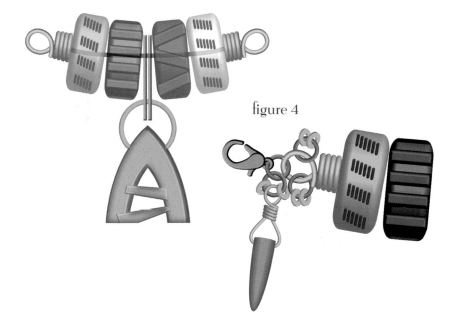

figure 4

1. Cut 4" (10.2 cm) of brass wire. String one bullet bead and slide it to the center of the wire. Bend the wire ends up, crossing them about ¹⁄₃" (8 mm) above the bullet bead.

2. Use one wire end to form a wrapped loop around both wires **(figure 1)**. Trim the excess wires **(figure 2)**. Set aside. Repeat to make a total of 14 bullet dangles.

3. Open one jump ring. Add one heishi, one bullet dangle, and one heishi. Close the ring and set it aside. Repeat to embellish all fourteen bullet dangles.

4. Form a wrapped loop at the end of the sterling silver wire. String on one green screw bead, one iron gear bead, the focal pendant, one zig wheel bead, and one oxidized screw bead. Form a wrapped loop to secure the beads. Gently bend the wire so it curves slightly upward **(figure 3)**.

5. Open one jump ring, add three heishi, and attach it to one of the sterling silver wrapped loops. Repeat to add a total of two beaded rings to each sterling silver wrapped loop.

6. Open one jump ring. Add one bullet dangle and one lobster clasp. Pass the open jump ring through one of the sterling silver wrapped loops between the beaded rings already placed **(figure 4)**.Close the jump ring. Repeat for the other sterling silver wrapped loop.

7. Open the first lobster clasp added in step 6. Attach a round steam gear link. Repeat for the second lobster clasp.

figure 5

8. Open one lobster clasp and add it to the other side of the first steam gear link placed in the previous step. Repeat for the second steam gear link.

9. Cut 4" (10.2 cm) of chain. Double the chain and use a jump ring to connect both end links to the first lobster clasp added in the previous step. Add a bullet dangle to the jump ring just added. Use a jump ring to connect a lobster clasp to the link at the fold (figure 5). Repeat for the second lobster clasp added in the previous step.

10. Working on the left side of the necklace, use a jump ring to attach a lobster clasp to the middle of the chain added in the previous step. Open the clasp and add the square compass charm. Move ½" (1.3 cm) down the chain to the left and add a bullet dangle.

11. Cut 4" (10.2 cm) of chain and double it. Open a jump ring and add both end links of the new chain and a lobster clasp. Add the jump ring to the leftmost lobster clasp already placed so the chain hangs vertically.

12. Use a jump ring to connect a lobster clasp to the link at the fold of the chain added in the previous step. Open the clasp and add a rust 6 × 25mm screw link. Open the jump ring of a bullet dangle and connect the chains about ½" (1.3 cm) from the last lobster clasp just placed (figure 6). Set aside.

13. String one fuchsia rondelle onto a head pin. Form a wrapped loop that attaches to the open end of the screw link added in the previous step (figure 7).

figure 7

figure 6

figure 8

figure 9

14. Open a jump ring and add the square porthole link, a pine screw link, and a bullet dangle. Close the ring. Use a jump ring to connect the pine screw link to the square timepiece link. Add a fuchsia rondelle dangle to the bottom of the timepiece link as you did in step 13. Hook the porthole link to the leftmost lobster clasp added in step 11.

15. Add a bullet dangle to the left loop of the porthole link. Set aside.

16. Cut 6" (15.2 cm) of chain. String the toggle bar on the chain and slide it to the center. Fold the chain, doubling it. Use the jump ring of a bullet dangle to connect the two sides of the chain 1" (2.5 cm) from the toggle bar. Open another jump ring and connect the chains ¾" (1.9 cm) from the ring just placed. Before closing the ring, attach it to the left loop of the porthole link. Use jump rings to attach one lobster clasp to each end of the chain **(figure 8)**.

17. String the square bolt bead onto a head pin; form a wrapped loop to secure the bead and set aside. Repeat with the round bolt bead. Attach one dangle to each of the lobster clasps placed in the previous step.

18. Working on the right side of the necklace, repeat step 10, substituting the motor oil keyhole link for the compass charm. Repeat steps 11–13 substituting the iron screw link for the rust one and a teal rondelle for the fuchsia one. Repeat step 14, replacing the oxidized keyhole link for the porthole link, the moss screw link for the pine one, the buckle link for the timepiece link, and a teal rondelle for a fuchsia one. Add a bullet dangle to the right loop of the keyhole link. Set aside.

19. Double the remaining 5" (12.7 cm) of chain. Drop the folded end of the chain into the center of the toggle ring. Open the fold to make a chain loop and bring the loop up and over the sides of the ring. Pull tight to make a knot **(figure 9)**.

20. Open a bullet dangle and connect the chains ¾" (1.9 cm) from the toggle ring.

21. Open a jump ring and connect the right loop of the keyhole link and the chains, ½" (1.3 cm) from the ends. Use jump rings to attach one lobster clasp to each end of the chain.

22. Open the first lobster clasp just placed and add the round steam gear charm. Open the second lobster clasp and attach the green screw charm.

Steampunk on Stage

With its roots solidly in the fantasy and science fiction worlds, Steampunk is theatrical by nature. Put on a Steampunk costume, and you'll soon find out. Archaic terms from the Old World seem to naturally roll off the tongue, and you'll suddenly find you've developed an itch for fiddling around with the time/space continuum.

Steampunk's built-in drama makes fertile ground for live theater, whose directors, costumers, and set designers work with every visual opportunity to set a performance's tone or convey a message. The 2008 production of Thomas Kilroy's *The Secret Fall of Constance Wilde* at the Guthrie Theater in Minneapolis is a perfect example. Costume designer Paul Tazewell outfitted the swirling, dark, silent characters in an extreme Steampunk style. These characters' costumes are Victorian in design, but deconstructed, like the emotions they represent.

Apsara is a San Francisco-based "living art" troupe that combines dance movements, fashion, props, music, video, and fire performance to tell stories and create moodscapes. These underground performance artists use their shows to "reinvent culture and art history," creating a venue in which the audience can dream and find inspiration. Here the troupe is pictured in their Steampunk-inspired costume, reminiscent of performers in a surreal nineteenth-century burlesque.

Apsara Living Art Troupe

Photo: Spencer Hansen

FINISHED LENGTH: 19" (48.3 cm)

TECHNIQUES: Coiling, simple loop, flush-cutting, opening/closing rings

Machinery in Motion
NECKLACE

DESIGNER: Melanie Brooks

Coiled wire dips and dives around metal rings and porcelain cogs, evoking the elaborate inner workings of a machine. The necklace itself, however, is anything but cold and mechanical —it's sheer beauty.

Materials and tools

* 6 × 8mm natural brass cable chain (10½" [26.7 cm])
* 5mm natural brass jump rings (26)
* 21.5mm natural brass hammered rings with drill holes (2)
* 3 × 10mm pointed dangles (2)
* 9mm natural brass etched jump rings (7)
* 20mm oxidized round porcelain gear links (4)
* 20mm oxidized round porcelain gear charm (1)
* 7mm natural brass jump rings (3)
* 6.5 × 24mm natural brass bead pod toggle bar (1)

* 3mm natural brass cube beads (9)
* natural brass-colored 22-gauge copper wire (72" [1.8 m])
* 1½" (3.8 cm) natural brass eye pins (4)
* chain-nose pliers (2)
* wire cutters
* coiling tool
* round-nose pliers

1. Cut the chain into two 5¼" (13.3 cm) pieces.

2. Open one 5mm jump ring and connect one end of one chain segment to the hole of one hammered ring. Before closing the jump ring, string on one dangle (**figure 1**).

figure 1

figure 2

cube on 5mm jump — — 2 5mm jumps

3. Use two 5mm jump rings to connect the other end of the chain segment from step 2 to an etched jump ring. Use two 5mm jump rings to connect the etched jump ring to one gear link. Continue using two 5mm jump rings to connect components in this order: one etched jump ring, one gear link, and one etched jump ring. Use one 7mm jump ring to connect the last etched jump ring placed to the center hole of the remaining hammered ring. Repeat this step in reverse, connecting to one end of the second chain segment.

4. Use two 5mm rings to connect the end of the second chain segment to the toggle bar.

5. Use one 5mm jump ring to connect one brass dangle to the small hole in the center hammered ring so the dangle sits in the middle of the ring.

6. Use one 7mm jump ring to connect one etched jump ring to center hole of the center hammered ring, opposite the brass dangle. Use two 5mm jump rings to connect the gear charm to the etched ring just placed. Open one 5mm jump ring, string one cube bead, and attach to the two jump rings just placed (**figure 2**). Set aside the chain.

7. Cut the wire into two 36" (0.9 m) pieces. Use the small winding rod of the coiling tool to create a coil with the first piece of wire, following the manufacturer's directions. Repeat with the remaining wire.

8. Use the wire cutters to cut five 1" (2.5 cm) pieces of coil. Set aside.

figure 3

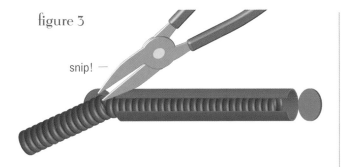

snip! —

9. Insert one of the coils into the toggle bar. Trim the coil so it fits neatly inside the bar **(figure 3)**. Close the ends of the bar to secure the coil.

10. String one cube bead, one 1" (2.5 cm) coil, and one cube bead onto an eye pin. Use round-nose pliers to form a simple loop, securing the beads and coil in place. Gently bend the wire and coil to form a half-circle wide enough to rest between the two loops of a gear link. Adjust the wire so the loops are parallel **(figure 4)**. Repeat to make a total of four coil links.

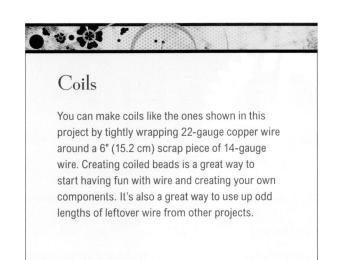

Coils

You can make coils like the ones shown in this project by tightly wrapping 22-gauge copper wire around a 6" (15.2 cm) scrap piece of 14-gauge wire. Creating coiled beads is a great way to start having fun with wire and creating your own components. It's also a great way to use up odd lengths of leftover wire from other projects.

figure 4

11. Attach the loops of one coil link to the loops of one gear link on the same side of the necklace that the gear charm sits **(figure 5)**. Repeat to add one coil link to each gear link.

figure 5

At the
Movies

Steampunk films are gloriously visual. The stories, usually centered around magical journeys with a sci-fi slant, are populated by quixotic heroes, wicked scoundrels, lash-fluttering ingénues, mad scientists, and usually some out-of-control monster or machine. The settings are moody, with nineteenth-century details galore: dark and rainy cobblestone back alleys; buzzing and crackling secret laboratories; and ramshackle decks of pirated flying machines. The costuming is grand, featuring the rich styling of Victorian fashion, accented with a post-apocalyptic tinker's assortment of found objects, weapons, and talismans.

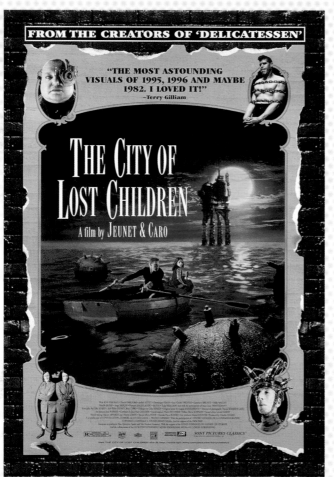

Photo: Sony Pictures Classics/Photo Fest

La Cité des Enfants Perdus ("The City of Lost Children"), a 1995 film made by Jean-Pierre Jeunet and Marc Caro, exemplifics Steampunk cinema in both its plot and art direction. The story follows a mad scientist who steals children's dreams and the strongman hero who fights to get them back. Villains sport monocles, and a set of conjoined twins, in the mold of Charles Dickens's famous Fagin, operate an orphanage and black-market business. Angelo Badalamenti's music is haunting, and the signature costuming of Jean Paul Gaultier is beyond your wildest dreams.

The Steampunk genre is not new to cinema. Some claim that one of Hollywood's first movies, *Metropolis* (1927) had many of the signature elements of modern Steampunk films: the theme of man vs. machine, the relationships of robots and mad scientists, social hierarchy issues, and the notion that the underdog should win. The idea of incorporating retro-futuristic Victorian-era stylings may have started with Disney's *20,000 Leagues Under the Sea,* based on the Jules Verne novel by the same name. The film features a strapping hero (Kirk Douglas), Captain Nemo's fantastical submarine (the *Nautilus*), and a giant squid. This neo-Victorian angle took hold in Hollywood, leading to later films such as *The Great Race, Chitty Chitty Bang Bang,* and *Willy Wonka & The Chocolate Factory.* This long tradition has continued, producing an explosion of Steampunk-influenced cinema in recent years with films like *League of Extraordinary Gentlemen, The Prestige,* and *The Golden Compass.*

Steampunk Style Films

20,000 Leagues Under the Sea (1954)

Around the World in 80 Days (1956, 2004)

Atlantis: The Lost Empire (2001)

Chitty Chitty Bang Bang (1968)

Dark City (1998)

The Golden Compass (2007)

The Great Race (1965)

Hellboy (2004)

La Cité des Enfants Perdus
("The City of Lost Children") (1995)

League of Extraordinary Gentlemen (2003)

*Lemony Snicket's A Series of
Unfortunate Events* (2004)

Perfect Creature (2006)

The Prestige (2006)

The Rocketeer (1991)

Sky Captain and the World of Tomorrow
(2004)

Stardust (2007)

The Time Machine (2002)

Treasure Planet (2002)

Wild Wild West (1999)

Willie Wonka & the Chocolate Factory (1971)

Van Helsing (2004)

Horological Faery Gadget necKlace

DESIGNER: Jen Hilton

fINISHED LENGTH: 18" (45.7 cm)

TECHNIQUES: coiling, flush-cutting, simple loop, opening/closing rings

In this magical necklace, a kinetic fairy with fluttering wings made from watch parts hovers gracefully along the links of a bright brass chain.

Materials and tools

* 20-gauge brass craft wire (12" [30.9 cm])
* 16 × 32mm bridges from disassembled pocket watches (2)
* 10 × 34mm pewter woman charm (1)
* 1" (2.5cm) brass head pins (2)
* 6mm antiqued brass bike-style chain (16" [40.6 cm])
* 2" (5.1 cm) brass head pin with ball end (1)
* sterling silver 5mm seamless round bead (1)

* 5 × 6mm antiqued brass cable chain (1¼" [3.2 cm])
* 18-gauge 6mm antiqued brass jump rings (2)
* 7 × 12mm antiqued brass lobster clasp (1)
* watchmaker's screwdrivers
* round-nose pliers
* wire cutters

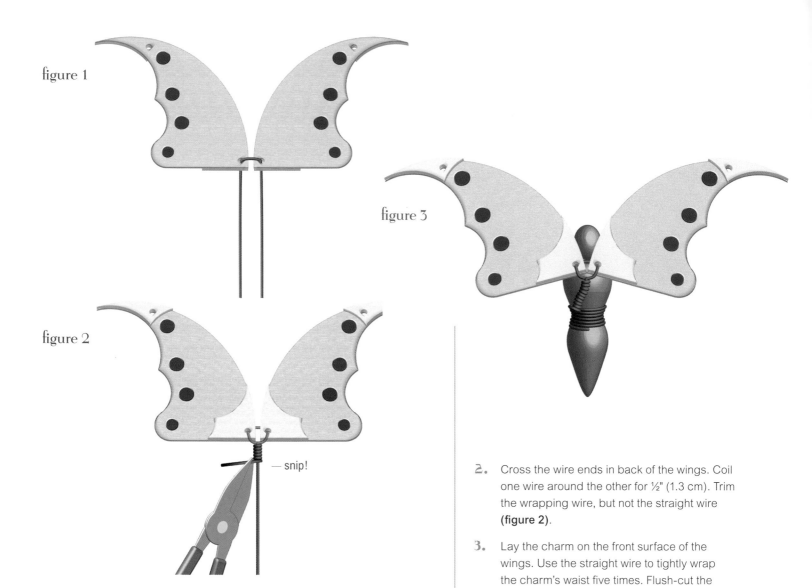

figure 1

figure 2

figure 3

— snip!

1. Use round-nose pliers to bend the middle of the wire to form a boxy U shape. The bent wire corners should be just far enough apart that when you pass the wire ends through the inner holes of the bridges from front to back, the inner edges of the "wings" just barely touch **(figure 1)**. The wings should move freely along the wire.

2. Cross the wire ends in back of the wings. Coil one wire around the other for ½" (1.3 cm). Trim the wrapping wire, but not the straight wire **(figure 2)**.

3. Lay the charm on the front surface of the wings. Use the straight wire to tightly wrap the charm's waist five times. Flush-cut the wire close to the wrap on the charm's back **(figure 3)**.

4. Manipulate the wirework so the head is upright and positioned properly between the wings.

5. Pass one 1" (2.5 cm) head pin through a hole at the tip of one wing from front to back. Pull tight and cut the head pin to ¼" (6mm) from the wing. Use round-nose pliers to form a simple loop. Repeat for the other wing tip.

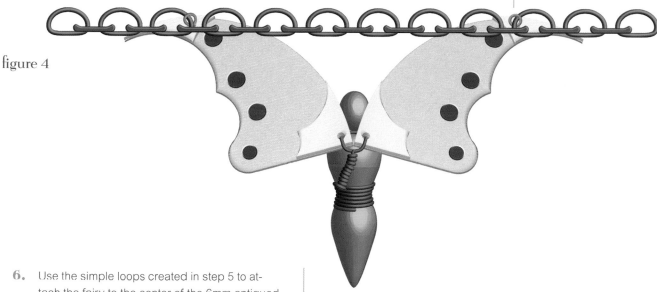

headpin loops connecting to chain

figure 4

6. Use the simple loops created in step 5 to attach the fairy to the center of the 6mm antiqued brass bike-style chain (**figure 4**). Set aside.

7. String the silver round bead onto the 2" (5.1 cm) head pin. Form a simple loop to secure the bead, but instead of trimming the wire tail, spiral it around the neck of the loop, down the edge of the bead, and around the ball tip (**figure 5**).

8. Open an end link of the 5 × 6mm cable chain and attach the dangle made in step 7. Close the link. Open the other end link of the cable chain and attach it to one end of the 6mm bike-style chain. Close the link.

9. Attach one jump ring to the lobster clasp. Use one jump ring to attach the jump ring just placed to the other end of the 6mm bike-style chain.

figure 5

Positioning the Wings

For the right effect, the watch bridges, or "wings," should be mirror images of each other. The bridges will need to have holes on either end so you can wire them to the fairy body and attach them to the chain. You may need to remove some small screws in order to use the holes.

Steampunk ANImATeD

The fantasy world of Steampunk is a natural fit for animation, a world in which anything is possible. Time-traveling dirigibles, football-field-sized steam-powered submarines, and out-of-control thingamajigs and whizbangs are easily brought into being with the stroke of a pen. There is a veritable imaginative feast in the imagery and storylines. Here are just a few of the animations with defining Steampunk elements:

The League of Extraordinary Gentlemen (1999) follows the adventures of a team of famous nineteenth-century characters, including Allan Quatermain, Captain Nemo, Dr. Henry Jekyll, and Mr. Edward Hyde. Creator Alan Moore is one of the masterminds behind the popularity of this graphic novel genre. Not only has he captured the imagination of readers, but he's also won over 20th Century Fox, which released a film of the same name in 2003.

Studio Foglio has swept the Steampunk comics world by storm with *Girl Genius,* the ongoing adventures of Agatha Heterodyne. This online graphic novel is set in an Industrial Revolution–era Europe ruled by rival mad scientists. Creators Phil and Kaja Foglio have filled their fictional world with fantastical laboratories and landscapes, trumped-up airships, crazed villains, and buxom ray-gun-toting, butt-kicking heroines. New pages of the novel appear three times a week on www.studiofoglio.com. The characters are often found in the flesh at cosplay events wearing colorful costume and accessories inspired by the whimsical minds of the Foglios.

Steamboy (2005) is a feature-length animated film by Katsuhiro Otomo. Originally released in Japan as *Suchîmubôi* in 2004, the movie is about an inventor prodigy, his experiments with steam-powered energy, and his ensuing fight against the forces of evil. This epic took the director ten years to make and is considered a great visual feat in animation, featuring both two- and three-dimensional effects.

From 1998 to 1999, the manga series *Steam Detectives* (*"Kaiketsu Jouki Tanteidan"*) quenched Tokyo fans' thirst for weekly installments of steam animation. The main characters—Narutaki, Lingling, and robot Gohliki—foil evil villains in Steam City, a sci-fi Victorian world covered with a steamy mist. The series is now available on DVD-ROM.

The Mysterious Geographical Explorations of Jasper Morello (2005) is an Academy Award–nominated film by Anthony Lucas. This simply breathtaking animated short features a dark, shadowy world menaced by a flesh-eating plague and is full of huge ironworked air buses and just enough Victoriana to transport viewers to the proper retro-future era.

Steampunk Animations

Castle in the Sky by Hayao Miyazaki
(feature-length film, 1986)

Cathedral Child by Lea Hernandez
(graphic novel series, 1998)

Fullmetal Alchemist by Hiromu Arakawa
(graphic novel and television series, 2001)

Girl Genius by Phil and Kaja Foglio
(graphic novel series, 2001)

Gotham by Gaslight by Brian Augustyn,
Mike Mignola, and P. Craig Russell
(graphic novel, 1989)

Iron West by Doug Ten Napel
(graphic novel, 2006)

The League of Extraordinary Gentlemen
by Alan Moore
(graphic novel series, 1999)

*The Mysterious Geographic Explorations of
Jasper Morello* by Anthony Luca
(animation, 2005)

Steamboy by Katsuhiro Otomo
(feature-length film, 2005)

Steam Detectives by Kia Asamiya
(television series, 1998)

FINISHED SIZE: 18mm ring top

TECHNIQUES: Gluing, flush-cutting

Airship Captain's
RING

DESIGNER: Jen Hilton

This bold ring features filigree, watch parts, and an articulated propeller charm. It's the perfect accessory to wear on the maiden flight of your steam-powered airship.

Materials and tools

* 2" (5.1 cm) brass headpin (1)
* 3mm watch gear with hole in its center (1)
* 5mm watch gear with hole in its center (1)
* 22mm brass propeller charm (1)
* 16 × 6mm brass filigree bead cap with 8 looped edges (1)
* 17mm brass pocket watch main-spring barrel (1)
* 18mm brass pocket watch main-spring barrel (1)
* brass ring base with flat 17mm round face and prongs (1)
* clear jeweler's adhesive
* safety glasses
* chain-nose pliers
* round-nose pliers
* flush cutters

Notes

* The bead cap featured in this design was purchased from a junk dealer at a flea market. The designer has no idea how old it is or if it was used as a bead cap, lamp pull cord, or wall fixture. As you shop for your ring's finding, look for any appropriately sized bead cap, making sure it has eight looped edges you can bend upward to make flat.

* When you reclaim the main-spring barrels from your pocket watches, you'll need to remove the mainsprings. Do so carefully with chain-nose pliers and be sure to wear safety glasses. This type of spring can unwind quickly, cut a hand or eye, or send the mainspring barrel flying!

figure 1

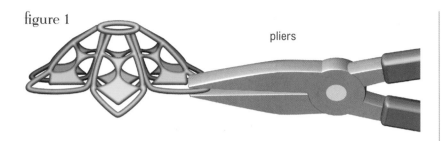

pliers

1. Using chain-nose pliers, gently bend the loops of the bead cap up toward the outside of the cap, creating a flat surface **(figure 1)**.

2. Cut the headpin to ¾" (19mm).

figure 2

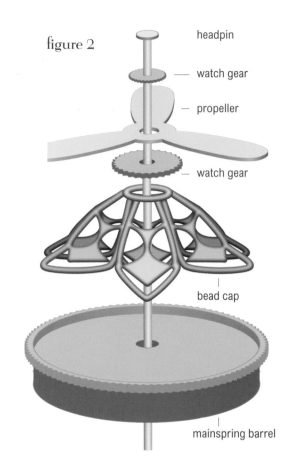

headpin

watch gear

propeller

watch gear

bead cap

mainspring barrel

3. String the following onto the headpin **(figure 2)**: the 3mm watch gear, the propeller charm, the 5.5mm watch gear, the bead cap (from outside to inside), and the 17mm mainspring barrel (from outside to inside).

Crash of the French military airship, *La Republic* on maneuvers. From a French weekly newspaper published in Paris, October 10, 1909.

4. Snug the components. Use chain-nose pliers to bend the headpin at a 90° angle. The bend should be flush against the inside of the mainspring barrel, holding the propeller and bead cap in place. Use round-nose pliers to form a small basic loop or coil that fits completely within the mainspring barrel **(figure 3)**.

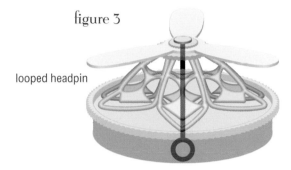

figure 3

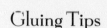

looped headpin

Gluing Tips

1. If a little bit of the jeweler's adhesive leaks while you're working, cut it away with a sharp craft knife or pull it away with a needle or tweezers. For this project, don't worry if the adhesive wells up through the hole in the 17mm mainspring barrel and around the head pin—it won't be very visible through the filigree bead cap.

2. If you happen to opt for a solid, not filigree, bead cap, fill the entire bead cap with jeweler's adhesive, too, just to hold it more securely. If the adhesive oozes out of the bottom of the 18mm barrel, just wipe or cut away the excess.

3. Steer clear of adding any adhesive between the propeller and the gear, or between the propeller and the bead cap. You want to be sure the propeller is able to turn when spun.

5. Fill the 17mm mainspring barrel with adhesive and set it inside the 18mm barrel. Press the barrels together. Allow it to dry until completely hardened.

6. Use adhesive to attach the bottom of the 18mm to the ring face **(figure 4)**. If necessary, bend the prongs down and out of the way. Let dry.

figure 4

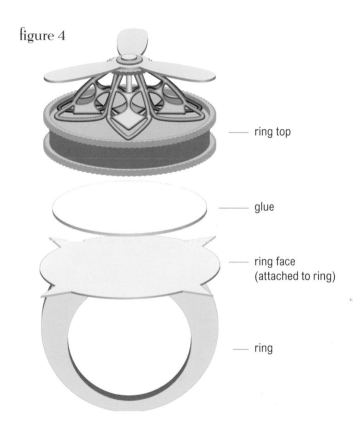

ring top

glue

ring face
(attached to ring)

ring

7. Use chain-nose pliers to bend the prongs upward and around the 18 mm mainspring barrel's gear teeth, further securing the ring top.

The Spirit of PLAY

Unlike other rebellious punk movements, Steampunk is rooted in a spirit of play, creativity, and experimentation. Xylocopa's *A Young Mad Scientist's First Alphabet Blocks* is a great example of the way Steampunk artists introduce an element of fun into everything they create or manipulate.

The designers at Xylocopa, alarmed at the lack of training for budding mad scientists in the public school system, have done their part to help preschoolers learn the essential terms of the trade, the entire alphabet from A (Appendages) to Z (Zombies). The anime-style illustrations and Old-World-type fonts, which are laser-engraved into the wood blocks, are pure Steampunk.

The same playful, whimsical quality is evident in another type of building-block play: the genius Lego sculptures of Hollywood special effects artist Guy Himber of V&A Steamworks. Working only with standard Lego pieces with an occasional Bionicle component thrown in, Himber combines the fun of the toy building bricks with the color palettes, shapes, and themes of Steampunk style.

Photo: Xylocopa

Xylocopa's *A Young Mad Scientist's First Alphabet Blocks*.

Kensington

Guy Himber's *HMS Vern.*

His HMS *Vern* conjures the image of a mechanical underwater beast, powered by steam and prepared, with its trusty crew, to go to blows with Jules Verne's underwater craft, the *Nautilus*.

Himber's *Kensington* is a pipe organ on steroids, with contraptions of all sorts ready to carry the evil top-hatted organist's haunting tune. Finally, the artist's signature steam engine, *Victoria*, whose driver is ready for post-apocalyptic travel, seems ready to blast through any time portal that it aims its small plastic smoke stack at.

Victoria

FINISHED SIZE: 26½" (67.3 cm)

TECHNIQUES: wrapped loop, flush-cutting, gluing, sawing, opening/closing rings

Dirigible Aviatrix
Necklace

DESIGNER: Barbe Saint John

In a time when few men were brave enough to pilot a dirigible, this woman happily sailed through the clouds. With a compass around your neck, your journey will always be true.

Materials and tools

* 4 × 11mm decorative long and short chain (16" [40.6 cm])
* 20-gauge brass wire (3' [0.9 m])
* 11mm metal washer (1)
* 5.5 × 4mm brass cog beads (12)
* 5 × 11mm brass tube beads (6)
* 19mm brass rings (2)
* 12 × 57mm brass hook-and-eye clasp (1)
* 47 × 58 × 3.5mm black vintage carved plastic oval belt buckle (1)
* 45 × 55mm image of female vintage aviator
* 45 × 55mm piece of mica tile
* 50 × 60mm piece of pink/gold/blue vintage stamped tin
* 5mm brass ⅛" (3.3mm) eyelets (2)
* ½" (13mm) miniature brass bolts (6)
* 4mm miniature brass nuts (6)
* 14-gauge 9mm brass jump rings (2)
* 16mm compass (1)
* 19mm brass bezel pendant setting (1)

* map paper
* wire cutters
* round-nose pliers
* chain-nose pliers
* jeweler's saw and size 1 blade
* bench pin
* sandpaper in 180- and 400-grits
* pencil
* scissors
* rawhide hammer
* thin permanent marker
* tin snips
* jeweler's needle files
* binder clips or clothespins
* dremel or flex shaft drill with ⅛" (3.3mm) and 1/16" (1.5mm) drill bits
* eyelet setter and steel block
* heavy duty wire cutters
* 5-minute two-part epoxy adhesive
* clear jeweler's adhesive/sealer
* brown or black acrylic paint

figure 1

1. Cut the chain into two 8" (20.3 cm) sections. Set aside.

2. Cut 4" (10.2 cm) of wire. Form a wrapped loop at one end that attaches to the metal washer **(figure 1)**.

3. String one cog bead, one tube bead, and one cog bead. Form another wrapped loop that attaches to a 19mm brass ring **(figure 2)**.

4. Cut 4" (10.2 cm) of wire. Form a wrapped loop at one end that attaches to the 19mm brass ring just placed. String one cog bead, one tube bead, and one cog bead. Form another wrapped loop that attaches to one end link of one chain.

5. Repeat step 4 to form a beaded link that connects the other end of the chain to one-half of the clasp.

figure 2

6. Repeat steps 2–5, attaching to the same washer to create the other half of the necklace.

7. Clamp one end of the saw blade in the saw and tighten the screw. Adjust the length of the saw frame if needed. Thread the other end of the saw blade through the buckle and tighten it to the frame.

8. Working on a bench pin, saw the center piece of the buckle at the end to remove it **(figure 3)**. Unscrew one end of the saw blade and remove from the buckle. Sand the cut areas smooth, first with 180- then 400-grit sandpaper. Set the buckle aside.

9. Select an image of a female pilot. If desired, add details like buildings and flying machines by employing cut-and-paste or digital collage techniques.

10. Lay the buckle over the image and move it around until you find a placement you like. Trace around the outside of the buckle with a pencil. Cut out the image with scissors.

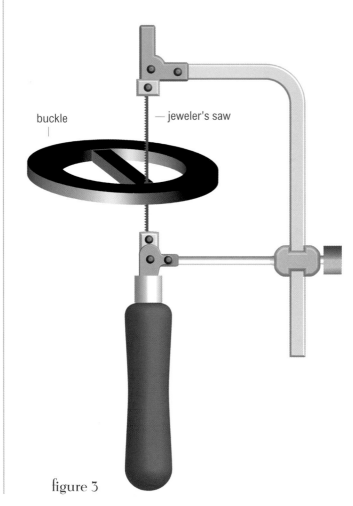

buckle — jeweler's saw

figure 3

II. Lay the belt buckle over the mica tile and trace around the outside of the buckle. Cut the shape with scissors and then set aside.

I2. If necessary, hammer the tin piece flat with a rawhide hammer. Lay the buckle on the tin and trace around the outside with a thin permanent marker. Cut the shape with tin snips and file smooth. Set aside.

I3. Place the tin cutout on the work surface, with the decorative side face down. Layer the pilot image, the mica cutout, and the buckle, so the buckle is on top **(figure 4)**. Check the placement of all the layers, making sure everything is straight and even. Use two or three binder clips or clothespins to carefully clamp the pieces so they are tightly in place.

I4. Use a permanent marker to make one mark at each end of the belt buckle, 1/3" (3.5 mm) from the end. These marks indicate the placement of the eyelets.

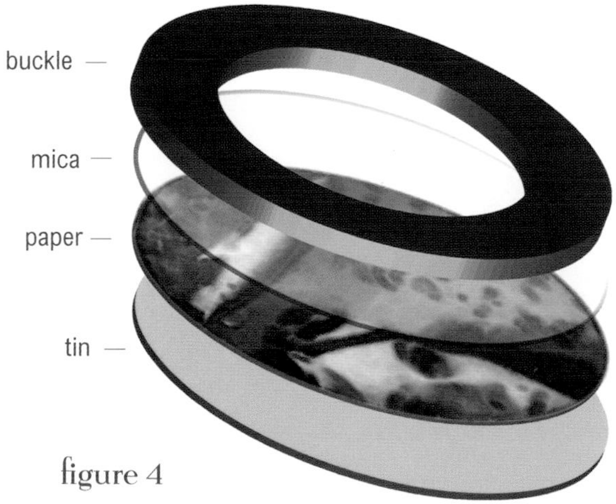

I5. Use the 1/8" (3.3mm) bit to drill the top hole. Add one eyelet and set it in place with the setter and hammer **(figure 5)**.

I6. Remove the clamps and check that all the layers are straight. Readjust if necessary and re-clamp the pendant. Drill the bottom eyelet hole and set the eyelet. Remove the clamps.

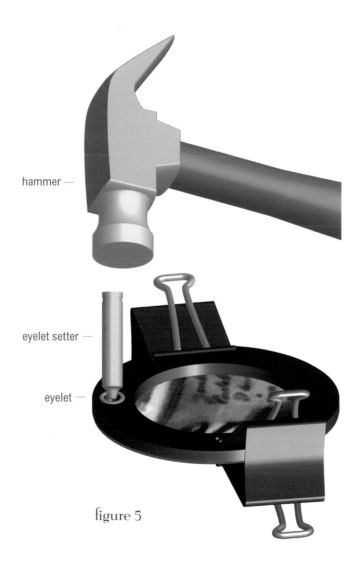

buckle —
mica —
paper —
tin —

figure 4

hammer —
eyelet setter —
eyelet —

figure 5

figure 6

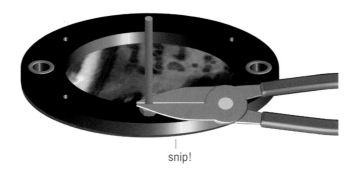

snip!

17. Use a permanent marker to mark three evenly spaced holes down each side of the buckle. Use the ¹⁄₁₆" (1.5mm) bit to drill out each hole. Pass one bolt through a hole from back to front. Add a nut and tighten. Use heavy-duty wire cutters to cut off any excess bolt length **(figure 6)**. File the bolt edges smooth. Repeat to add bolts and nuts to each of the holes.

18. Use a 9mm jump ring to connect the top of the pendant to the washer.

19. Use 180-grit sandpaper to lightly sand the bottom of the compass. Mix the two-part epoxy according to the manufacturer's directions and apply it to the bottom of the compass. Place the compass in the bezel setting and let it dry.

20. Trace the shape of the bezel back onto the map paper. Cut out the shape. Use the jeweler's adhesive/sealer to glue the paper to the back of the bezel. Let the glue dry.

21. Use a wash of brown or black paint to "age" the map and color the edges. Allow the paint to dry.

22. Mix a small amount of two-part epoxy and spread a thin layer over the map paper. Allow the glue to set.

23. Use a 9mm jump ring to connect the compass charm to the bottom of the pendant.

Maker's Tips

You can find nearly all the materials in this necklace at your local flea market. Sometimes the best things are hidden in the piles of broken junk that most people pass by. For example, rusty tins are no good for storing tea, but they're perfect to cut up for tin pieces. Someone may not want that gorgeous but cracked Bakelite belt buckle, but it's perfect for this project.

Personalize the pendant by adding a photo of a loved one. Scan the photo and change the tint to sepia or black and white with your computer's photo editing software. Choose map paper from his or her hometown or incorporate a bit of paper that has his or her handwriting. You could also use a scrap from a special piece of clothing—a bit of wedding-gown lace or fabric from a favorite shirt or tie.

Green
Steam

The Academy of Unnatural Science's *Neverwas Haul.*

Steampunk has an environmentally friendly bent. Many of the items used to create its fashion, accessories, gadgetry, and paraphernalia are recycled. The modern maker resembles the frenetic inventor or mad scientist at the center of Steampunk fiction, scrounging for equipment and spare parts in the laboratory to create an object that is totally new.

Innovative reuse is a key concept for Steampunk designers of all disciplines. Jewelry designers hunt flea markets to find skeleton keys, watch parts, and other small fabricated metals. Clothing designers scrounge thrift shops, looking for anything with decorative Victorian detailing, with an eye to take it apart, reassemble it, and turn it into a new fashion statement. Functional designers, who modify computers, cars, and guitars, prowl garage sales and scrap yards and even sometime engage in dumpster diving, or *binning.* All of these creative geniuses seem to prefer the challenge of revinventing lost treasures rather than simply buying new.

Neverwas Haul, a self-propelled Victorian house created by the Academy of Unnatural Sciences in Berkeley, California, is a great example of Steampunk makers utilizing found objects on a grand scale. This vehicle, which was originally built in 2006 for the *Burning Man Festival,* is made up of 75 percent recycled materials. It runs on alternative fuel, is outfitted with a camera obscura, tours the Steampunk festivals, and is actually available for rent as a venue for private events.

Voluminating Exhalator BRACELET

DESIGNER: Jamie Hogsell

Whirling wire coils and romantic filigree disks combine to make a decidedly steam-themed wireworked bracelet. The metallic and colored surfaces complement each other, adding depth and a bit of flair.

Materials and tools

* 26-gauge colored copper wire in dark blue, natural brass, and brown (one 30-yard [27.4 m] spool of each)
* 22-gauge colored copper wire in amethyst, dark blue, and natural brass (one 10-yard [9.1 m] spool of each)
* 23mm natural brass sparrow's compass filigree disk (8)
* 2" (5.1cm) natural brass head pins (8)
* 3mm natural brass melon beads (8)
* 3mm natural brass trade spacers (26)
* 10 × 14mm natural brass swirl hook clasp (1)

* 10mm natural brass 18-gauge jump ring (1)
* nylon-jaw pliers or wire straighteners
* small coiling tool
* wire cutters
* wire jig
* spiral-making tool
* round-nose pliers
* chain-nose pliers
* flat-nose pliers

1. Working directly from the spool (don't cut the wire), use nylon-jaw pliers to remove any kinks from a long length of dark blue 26-gauge wire. Following the manufacturer's directions, use the coiling tool to form a 2mm-wide coil 5" (12.7 cm) long. Trim the wire ends and use nylon-jaw pliers to curve the ends of the wire around the coiling tool. Remove the coil from the tool and set it aside. Repeat the process to make a total of three dark blue coils.

2. Repeat step 1 to make three natural brass and three brown coils.

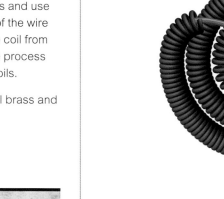

figure 1

working wire —

— tail wire

— blue coil

Coiling

Don't have a Coiling Gizmo, jig, or spiral maker? No problem. Although there are tools for these techniques that make the project go more quickly, you can easily make your own coils and spirals.

Coil: Tightly wrap the 22-gauge copper wire around a 10" (25.4cm) scrap of 20-gauge wire to the desired length. Flush-cut the ends and use nylon-jaw pliers to tuck the wire ends.

Spiral: Pass the 22-gauge wire through the coil as in step 3 of the project instructions. Grasp one end of the 22-gauge wire with round-nose pliers and form a simple loop. Grasp the loop so it lies flat within nylon-jaw pliers. Use your fingers to bend the 22-gauge wire alongside the loop. Adjust the position of the pliers and repeat the bending process to spiral the coiled wire along the loop.

3. Working from the spool, use nylon-jaw pliers to remove any kinks from a long length of amethyst 22-gauge wire. Use the amethyst wire to string 1 dark blue coil. Following the manufacturer's directions, use the jig and spiral maker to form a 15 to 20mm spiral, leaving a 2" (5.1 cm) tail. Wrap the working wire around the tail wire to secure, allowing the end of the coil to tuck slightly under the spiral (**figure 1**). Flush-cut the working end. Set aside. Repeat to make a total of three dark blue spirals.

4. Repeat step 3 to make three natural brass spirals, using dark blue 22-gauge wire as the base, and three brown spirals, using natural brass 22-gauge wire as the base.

5. Use the tail end of a brown spiral to pass through the right edge of one brass disk, from back to front. Wrap the tail end twice around the disk's edge to secure. Trim the tail (**figure 2**).

6. String one melon bead onto a head pin. Pass through the left side of one brass disk, from front to back. Pass through the center of the brown coiled spiral and the previous brass disk **(figure 3)**.

7. Bend the head pin at a 90° angle away from the center of the disk. String three trade spacers and form a wrapped loop parallel to the disks **(figure 4)**.

8. Repeat steps 5–7 with a dark blue spiral, connecting to the right side of the same disks. When forming the wrapped loop in step 7, make it perpendicular to the disks **(figure 5)**.

9. Repeat steps 5–7 with one natural brass spiral, attaching the wrapped loop to the previous wrapped loop. Repeat step 8 with one brown spiral.

10. Repeat step 9 with one blue spiral on the left and one natural brass spiral on the right.

11. Repeat step 9 with one brown spiral on the left and one blue spiral on the right.

12. Attach the clasp hook to the wrapped loop formed in step 7. Attach the jump ring to the last wrapped loop formed in step 11.

13. Use the tail wire of the remaining natural brass spiral to string two trade spacers. Form a wrapped loop that attaches to the jump ring.

14. Place the bracelet around the wrist. Gently curve each head pin to follow the wrist's curve.

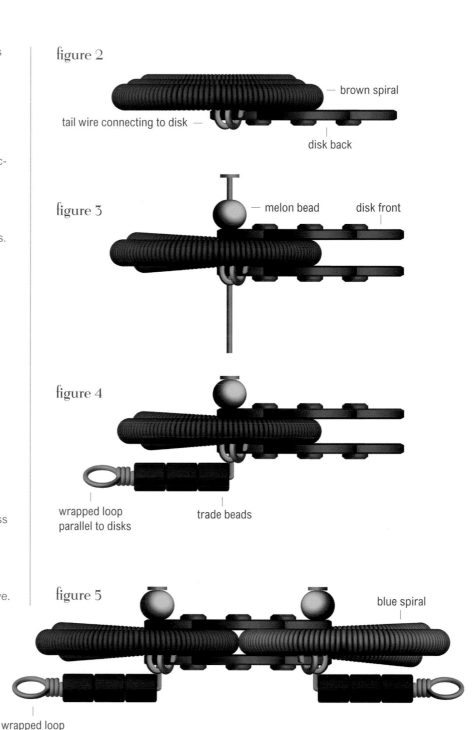

figure 2

brown spiral

tail wire connecting to disk —

disk back

figure 3

— melon bead   disk front

figure 4

wrapped loop
parallel to disks

trade beads

figure 5

blue spiral

wrapped loop
perpendicular to disks

Choosing Materials

Paging through the projects in this book, you'll get an overall sense of the materials appropriate for Steampunk-style jewelry, but there's much more history behind those choices than you might think. Steampunk materials have a lot in common with the materials jewelers used in the Victorian and Edwardian eras.

Metal findings and chain: With the advent of the Industrial Revolution, the middle class had sudden access to affordable pinchbeck (a golden copper/zinc alloy) and steel that were stamped, pressed, and rolled into chains. In Steampunk jewelry, brass and copper nod to the nineteenth century and add a Machine-Age look.

Charms: Queen Victoria is often credited with popularizing charm bracelets and necklaces, which have inherent sentimentality and personal symbolism. Charms are an important part of Steampunk jewelry, although the charms today—milagros, keys, watch parts, and textured and weathered found objects—have a different flavor than the charms of Victoria's time.

Glass: The Machine Age brought a leap in glass-manufacturing technology. Etching, faceting, and molding were finally possible and affordable. Today's jewelers use glass beads, cabochons, mirrors, and more to embellish their Steampunk creations.

Stones: The peace and prosperity of the burgeoning empire of mid-nineteenth-century England resulted in a trade boost with Asia. Ships were able to safely bring back gemstones to England. The types of stone that were suddenly available

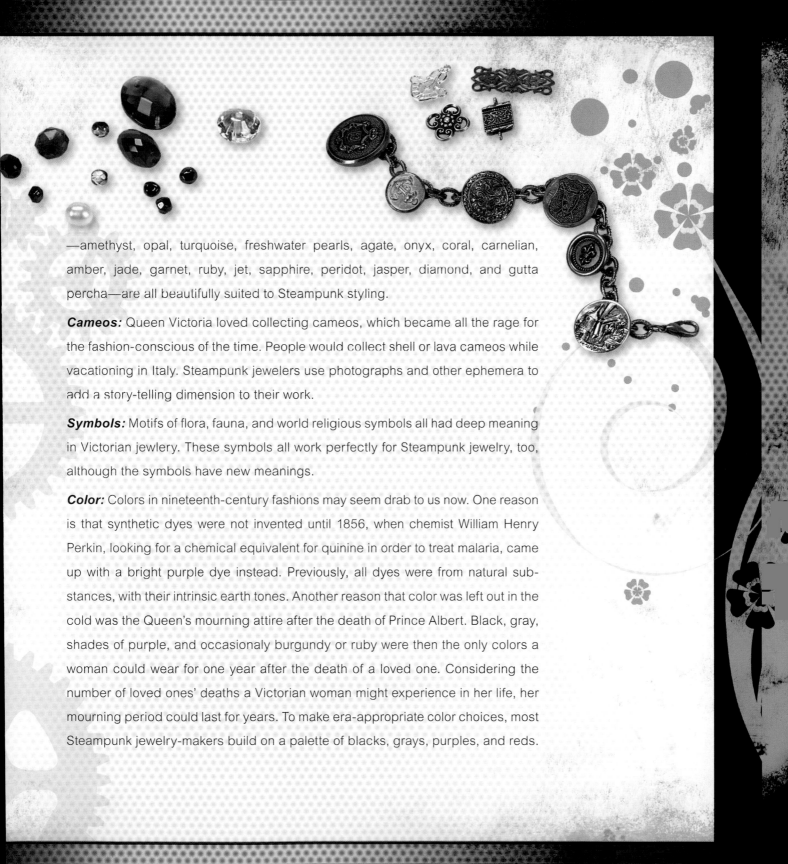

—amethyst, opal, turquoise, freshwater pearls, agate, onyx, coral, carnelian, amber, jade, garnet, ruby, jet, sapphire, peridot, jasper, diamond, and gutta percha—are all beautifully suited to Steampunk styling.

Cameos: Queen Victoria loved collecting cameos, which became all the rage for the fashion-conscious of the time. People would collect shell or lava cameos while vacationing in Italy. Steampunk jewelers use photographs and other ephemera to add a story-telling dimension to their work.

Symbols: Motifs of flora, fauna, and world religious symbols all had deep meaning in Victorian jewlery. These symbols all work perfectly for Steampunk jewelry, too, although the symbols have new meanings.

Color: Colors in nineteenth-century fashions may seem drab to us now. One reason is that synthetic dyes were not invented until 1856, when chemist William Henry Perkin, looking for a chemical equivalent for quinine in order to treat malaria, came up with a bright purple dye instead. Previously, all dyes were from natural substances, with their intrinsic earth tones. Another reason that color was left out in the cold was the Queen's mourning attire after the death of Prince Albert. Black, gray, shades of purple, and occasionaly burgundy or ruby were then the only colors a woman could wear for one year after the death of a loved one. Considering the number of loved ones' deaths a Victorian woman might experience in her life, her mourning period could last for years. To make era-appropriate color choices, most Steampunk jewelry-makers build on a palette of blacks, grays, purples, and reds.

Chronos #8
Necklace

DESIGNER: Madelyn Smoak

Vintage brass wings—
a WWII Technical
Observer Military
Grade lapel plaque,
to be exact—provided
the focal point for this
pendant necklace.
The wings worked
perfectly with the
vintage clockworks and
stamped number disk.

Materials and tools

* 8 × 2cm pair of brass wings (1)
* 34mm vintage pocket watch works (1)
* 32mm brass tag incised with the number 8 (1)
* 20-gauge copper wire (2" [5.1 cm])
* 5 × 7mm antiqued copper heavy rolo chain (18" [45.7 cm])
* 7mm copper split rings (4)
* 7 × 11mm copper lobster clasp (1)
* high-speed rotary craft drill with #52 twist drill bit
* scrap wood
* clear jeweler's adhesive
* rubber gloves

* liver of sulfur
* water
* plastic cup
* copper tongs
* 000 steel wool
* split-ring pliers
* round-nose pliers
* wire cutters

Working with Liver of Sulfur

Liver of sulfur, or sulfurated potash, is one of the patinas that jewelry artists use most often. It turns brass and silver black, giving these metals an antiqued look. Liver of sulfur is a very versatile patina. You can experiment with water temperature and soak time to achieve surprising green, blue, and purple finishes.

If you're going to work with liver of sulfur, don't be cavalier about handling it. This substance is extremely toxic when ingested, highly toxic when inhaled, and moderately toxic when it comes in contact with your skin. Be sure to work outdoors if possible. If you're working indoors, wear a respirator. Always don your rubber gloves so the solution doesn't come in contact with your skin.

When you've finished the antiquing process, don't toss used liver of sulfur down the sink. Instead, refer to the chemical hazard information sheet that's included with the product for information about how to dispose of the substance properly.

1. Place the wings on the scrap wood. Drill one hole in each of the top interior corners of the wings (figure 1).

2. Glue the bottom front of the wings to the top back of the watch works (figure 2). Allow the glue to dry for 24 hours. Check on the piece after 2 hours to make sure the parts didn't shift.

3. When the glue is completely dry, check to see whether the watch has a hole at the 6 o'clock position, 2 mm from the edge. If not, place the works on the scrap wood and drill a hole. Set aside.

4. Working outdoors or wearing a respirator, prepare the liver of sulfur solution in the plastic cup according to the manufacturer's directions. Put on the rubber gloves and use the copper tongs to dip the brass tag in the solution and let soak until it turns black. Remove the tag with copper tongs and rinse it well with water. Burnish the tag with steel wool until it has the desired patina. Set aside the tag.

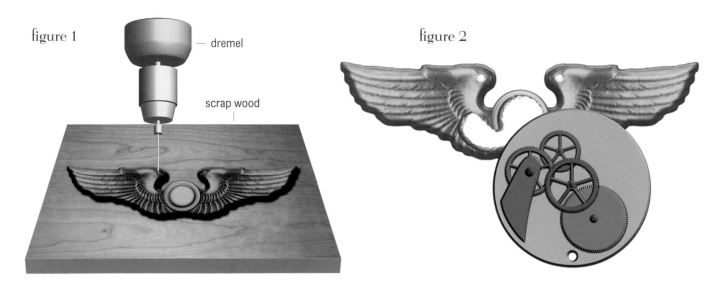

figure 1

— dremel

scrap wood

figure 2

figure 3

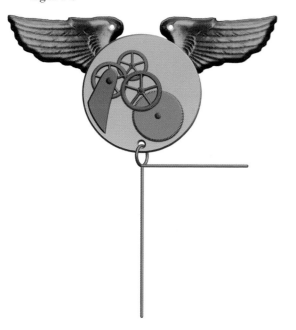

figure 4

figure 5

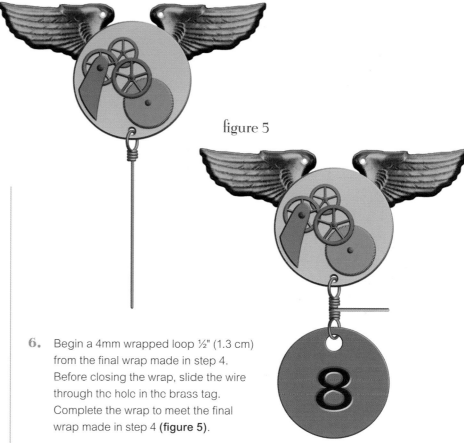

5. Begin a 4mm wrapped loop at one end of the wire. Before closing the wrap, slide the wire through the hole at the bottom of the watch works **(figure 3)**. Wrap the wire three times around the stem. Flush-cut the tail wire and use chain-nose pliers to tuck the wire end close to the stem **(figure 4)**.

Safety Tip

The fumes from a clear jeweler's adhesive like E-6000 or epoxy are very toxic. Work with these products outdoors, or wear a respirator if you're working indoors.

6. Begin a 4mm wrapped loop ½" (1.3 cm) from the final wrap made in step 4. Before closing the wrap, slide the wire through the hole in the brass tag. Complete the wrap to meet the final wrap made in step 4 **(figure 5)**.

7. Cut the chain into two 9" (22.9 cm) segments.

8. Use split-ring pliers to open one split ring. Use the split ring to connect one end of one chain to the hole in one of the wings. Repeat the process for the second chain segment and other wing.

9. Use split-ring pliers to open one split ring. Use the split ring to connect one end of one chain to the clasp.

10. Use split-ring pliers to open one split ring. Attach the split ring to the remaining chain end.

Steampunk sculpture

Like the tinkerers who mod common items or jewelry-makers who incorporate found objects into their finished pieces, Steampunk sculptors use bits of everyday life to create three-dimensional works of art. Their methods and results are as varied as the makers themselves—sometimes whimsical and humorous, sometimes dark and thought-provoking.

Belgian sculptor Stephane Halleux seems to pluck Steampunk characters right off the page, brand them with whimsy and surrealism, and transform them into extraordinary works of art. He combines metal odds and ends with all manner of hardware, leather, and minimally carved hands and faces to create figures that look as though they are about to get up and walk away. His *Beauty Machine* portrays a retro-futuristic salon chair that looks a bit more like a torture device than seating in a spa.

Artist Keith Newstead, of Cornwall, England, specializes in all types of colorful and whimsical automata. When he discovered Steampunk, he fell in love with the imagery and was inspired to make a special piece called *Steampunk*. This hand-cranked kinetic sculpture, made with old alarm clocks, car inner tubes, empty oil cans, and fencing wire, has wings that flap up and down, wheels that spin, and

Keith Newstead,
Steampunk

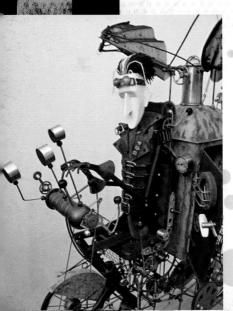

Photo: Keith Newstead

Photo: Kathy Chapman

Gina Kamentsky,
100 Turns is Heavy

Barbe Saint John,
Baby New Year 1898

a driver that rocks back and forth as his hands operate the steering equipment.

Gina Kamentsky has been creating her "mechanical confections" from industry scraps for twenty years. Her automata and kinetic sculpture explore the ideas of movement, gesture, memory, work, and value. Kamentsky doesn't consider herself a Steampunk artist per se, but her work informs and inspires others who identify more closely with the genre. In her wind-up sculpture, *100 Turns is Heavy,* Kamentsky used alternative materials to act as gears and cogs, resulting in a mechanized and whimsical version of what might be a post-modern alarm clock.

In *Sympathy,* Australian artist Julia DeVille combines taxidermy with found objects to create a sculpture that celebrates both life and death. DeVille's work, which often incorporates animals that have died of natural causes, is directly inspired by Victorian mourning jewelry. Following that tradition, she chooses her materials to create memento mori, or reminders of our mortality.

San Franciscan Barbe Saint John, of Saints and Sinners, creates her Steampunk assemblages with a wide array of found objects. *Baby New Year 1898* includes a clock, doll parts, and various scrap metal pieces to create the visage of a post-apocalyptic Victorian-Era icon. (See more of Saint John's work on pages 34 and 102.)

Julia DeVille, *Sympathy.*

Stephane Halleux,
Beauty Machine.

Tick Tock Drop
Earrings

designer: Melanie Brooks

These dramatic earrings, made from an unlikely pairing of mismatched clock hands and gear-textured porcelain beads, reinvent and make the most of their individual components.

Materials and tools

* 13 × 58mm black metal clock hands (2)
* 6 × 8 natural brass filigree tubes (2)
* 15mm oxidized round porcelain gear charms (2)
* 5mm natural brass jump rings (10)
* 7mm natural brass jump rings (2)
* 4 × 2.5mm natural brass spacer beads (2)
* natural brass ear wires (2)
* fine metal file
* chain-nose pliers (2 pairs)

figure 1

1. If necessary, use the metal file to remove any rough areas of the clock hands. Set aside the hands.

2. Use chain-nose pliers to slightly open a filigree tube at the seam. Insert one clock hand into the tube above the flared tip part of the hand.

3. Adjust the tube so the seam is on the back of the hand. Gently squeeze the tube around the clock hand, overlapping the tube ends **(figure 1)**. Make sure the tube's edges are folded so they are as flush as possible. Set aside.

4. Use two pairs of chain-nose pliers to attach two 5mm jump rings to one gear charm.

Clock Hands

Clock hands are a great resource for jewelry design. They come in a wide variety of fancy shapes and sizes and are often inexpensive. They are made of very thin, lightweight material, so they are the perfect choice for earrings. You can also easily cluster several of them in a design.

5. Open one 5mm jump ring and string one spacer bead on it. Attach the ring to the two 5mm jump rings you placed in step 4 **(figure 2)**.

6. Attach one 5mm jump ring to the two 5mm jump rings placed in step 4. Place this ring so the ring you placed in step 5 falls on the front of the charm.

7. Use one 7mm jump ring to attach the 5mm jump ring placed in step 6 to the top loop of one of the clock hands **(figure 3)**.

8. Use one 5mm jump ring to attach the 7mm jump ring you placed in step 7 to one ear wire.

9. Repeat steps 2–8 to make the second earring.

figure 2

— spacer bead

— 5mm jumps

— steam charm

figure 3

— 7mm ring

Steampunk
COUTURE

A piece from Hermes'
Fall 2009 collection.

The core concept of Steampunk fashion design is to juxtapose Victorian styling and punk attitude. This brand of "tattered couture" has been in high fashion's bag of tricks for years. The Steampunk version of this approach pairs "high" and "low" fashion—the perfect way to create elegant runway couture with the requisite elements of surprise, edginess, and modernity.

Vivienne Westwood, a premier fashion designer for the punk rock movement, was one of the first couture designers to start experimenting with high/low style. Her 1981 Pirate collection was a mix of swashbuckling silhouettes and punk-style-inspired color and fabrics. Westwood has continued to experiment with mixing these sensibilities, and her Spring/Summer 2009 Anglomania collection is no exception (www.viviennewestwood.com).

The Hermes Fall 2009 collection features carefully tailored bomber jackets, trench coats, and short evening dresses, paired with flight helmets, goggles, and punk-style riveted belts, thigh-high leather boots, and corset-style heels. The fabrics and texture are mixed—leather, fur, silk, knitwear— for a very Victorian aesthetic.

John Galliano's Fall 2009 collection, a conglomeration of many classic eras of fashion, features models sporting greatly exaggerated bustles and large gearlike buttons connected by chain on just about every ensemble—most decidedly Steampunk.

Custom-made Rhinestone Tiger Tutu Party Dress, New York Couture.
Photo credit: Steve Prue, Model: Alex, Hair stylist: Kristin Jackson, Makeup: Daniel Koninsky
The silhouette of this theatrical New York Couture party dress evokes the romance of a nineteenth-century ballerina,and the custom rhinestone tiger and hand-painted tulle adds punk style.

Tempus Fugit pendant

DESIGNER: Tracy Thomasson

FINISHED LENGTH: 30 × 42mm (small) and 35 × 47mm (large)

TECHNIQUES: Gluing, opening/closing rings

This pocket watch pendant won't tell you the time, but its appeal is timeless. It's made with a little clear epoxy resin, a layered collage of old watch parts, small charms, and some patience.

Materials and tools

* 30 × 42mm or 35 × 47mm antiqued brass pocket watch locket (1)
* jewelry-grade two-part epoxy resin
* 12–15mm antiqued brass charm (1)
* assorted 3mm–10mm watch parts (12–20)
* 3 × 5mm antiqued brass flat cable chain (16" [40.6 cm])
* 3.5 × 5mm antiqued brass oval jump rings (3)
* 4 × 6mm antiqued brass oval jump rings (2)
* 6 × 12mm antiqued brass lobster clasp (1)
* plastic cling wrap
* latex gloves
* disposable plastic medicine cups (like those used for cough syrup)
* several wooden coffee stirrers or bamboo skewers
* fine tweezers
* wire cutters
* chain-nose pliers

1. Lay out a layer of cling wrap on a table in a well-ventilated area where your project can remain undisturbed for twenty-four hours.

2. Take apart the pocket watch locket and lay it face down on the table. Set aside the backing.

3. Put on the latex gloves. Following the manufacturer's directions, mix together about two teaspoons of two-part resin in a plastic medicine cup. Completely mix the resin with a coffee stirrer.

4. Pour a thin layer of resin into the pocket watch locket, filling it to about one-third of the way full **(figure 1)**.

5. Use tweezers and a coffee stirrer to place the charm face down in the resin. Begin adding a few watch gears and other watch parts around the charm, but don't fully cover the face of the locket **(figure 2)**. If you put too many pieces in this first layer, you won't get a nice three-dimensional effect. Let the first layer of resin set for at least five hours.

6. Check the hardness of the resin by gently poking it with a coffee stirrer. It should no longer be liquid, but should still be tacky. It's okay if the stirrer presses into the resin a bit. If the resin is still wet, allow it to set up a bit longer.

7. Mix another small batch of resin in a new medicine cup with a new coffee stirrer. (Using the old stirrer might upset the epoxy ratio and keep it from setting up.) Pour the second layer of resin into the locket so that it's about two-thirds full. Repeat step 5 to add another layer of watch parts. Focus on filling the gaps you left in the first layer **(figure 3)**. Let this layer cure for at least eight hours.

figure 1

figure 2

8. Mix a third batch of resin and pour it into the locket, filling it to the top. Leave the piece overnight to cure.

9. When the resin is completely set, place the back onto the locket.

10. Cut the chain into two 8" (20.3 cm) pieces. Set aside.

11. Connect two 3.5 × 5mm jump rings to the top of the locket. Use one 4 × 6mm jump ring to attach one end of each chain to the two 3.5 × 5mm jump rings you just placed **(figure 4)**.

12. Use one 3.5 × 5mm jump ring to attach the clasp to one end of the chain. Attach one 4x6mm jump ring to the other end of the chain.

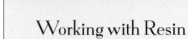

Working with Resin

If your resin remains tacky and doesn't fully set up after twelve hours, try adding a very thin layer of *just* the hardener to your project. Give the project another eight to twelve hours of dry time, and you should be good to go.

figure 3

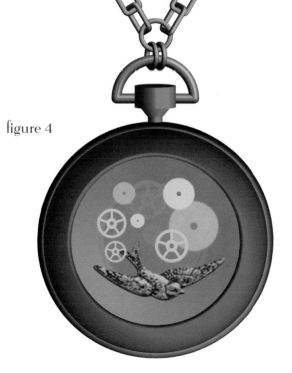

figure 4

Goggles
Galore

A pair of goggles is a must-have for a proper Steampunk ensemble. You never know when you might be invited on a time-traveling adventure, and you certainly don't want sparks to get in your eyes while experimenting in your lab. Some Steampunk fashion followers visit surplus stores to buy vintage WWII goggles. Others grab the off-the-shelf versions from welding supply stores. There are also a whole host of artists who just create their own.

Melanie Brooks, owner of Earthenwood Studio and all-around Steampunk guru, fashioned these all-purpose time traveling/mad scientist goggles for herself to wear at the many costuming and artist fairs she attends. She started with a plain pair of goggles she bought through Studio Foglio's website. She then modded the googles to add bolts, nuts, Ultrasuede, brass birds, and purse hardware.

Artist Rob Powell painted a pair of plastic athletic glasses with bronze paint to create a starting point for these all-seeing goggles. He then incorporated several lenses and the strap from

Photo: Melanie Brooks

Melanie Brooks. *Steampunk Goggles.*

128

Rob Powell. *Steampunk Goggles.*

an old Polaroid camera, watch parts and bezels, the gears from an antique wind-up alarm clock, and filigree from an old brass light fixture.

Nicholas Chambon's Atomefabrik studio in north London handcrafts a wide array of Steampunk and cyber-style accessories, but the goggles—oh, the goggles! His *steammachinegunner goggles* are made of machined brass, stainless hardware (nuts, bolts, cable), steel piano wire, brass wire, leather (sheep skins and cow skins), high-strength aluminum alloy, and acrylic (Perspex).

Nicholas Chambon.
Steammachinegunner Goggles.

fINISHED LENGTH: 7½" (19.1 cm)

TECHNIQUES: Wrapped loop, flush-cutting, gluing, opening/closing rings

Admiral's Secret
cuff

DESIGNER: Jean Campbell

A simple leather cuff meets brass eyelet embellishments, elaborate shiny brass filigree findings, and a smattering of pearls. The result? An easy project with official naval flair for first-time leather workers.

Materials and tools

* acrylic sealer
* 13 × 18mm vintage photo (1)
* clear dimensional adhesive
* 13 × 18mm clear glass cabochon (1)
* clear jeweler's adhesive
* 15 × 20mm brass locket (1)
* 8 × 20mm brass ribbon crimps (2)
* brown 2 × 13 cm piece of textured leather (1)
* 6mm brass eyelets (4)
* 1" (2.5 cm) brass ball-end head pins (6)
* white 6mm freshwater potato pearls (6)
* 5 × 6mm brass oval jump rings (8)
* 16 × 24mm shiny brass three-hole filigree connectors (4)

* 16 × 25mm brass D ring (1)
* toothpicks
* flat-nose pliers
* ruler
* pen
* scrap wood
* high-speed craft drill with 2mm bit
* eyelet setter
* hammer and block
* chain-nose pliers
* round-nose pliers
* wire cutters

1. Cover the photo, front and back, with acrylic sealer. Let dry.

2. Use your finger to apply a layer of dimensional adhesive to the back of the cabochon. Apply the photo so the image appears through the front. Press out any bubbles. Add more dimensional adhesive to the back of the photo. Allow the adhesive to dry completely.

3. Use a toothpick to apply a layer of jeweler's adhesive to the front of the locket. Press the back of the cabochon into the adhesive **(figure 1)**. Set aside to dry.

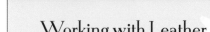

Working with Leather

You can buy inexpensive scrap leather at surplus stores and craft stores. If you can't find textured leather, add texture of your own with a craft iron or simply stamp the leather with permanent ink to make faux texture.

figure 1

4. Place one ribbon crimp over one end of the leather. Use flat-nose pliers to squeeze the crimp in place. Repeat to add the second ribbon crimp to the other end of the leather **(figure 2)**.

5. Use a ruler and pen to mark four evenly spaced holes lengthwise down the center of the leather. Lay the leather on the scrap wood and drill holes at each mark.

6. Use the eyelet setter, hammer, and block to set one eyelet in each hole in the leather **(figure 3)**. Set aside the leather.

7. Use one head pin to string one pearl. Form a wrapped loop to secure the pearl. Set aside. Repeat to make a total of six pearl dangles.

figure 2

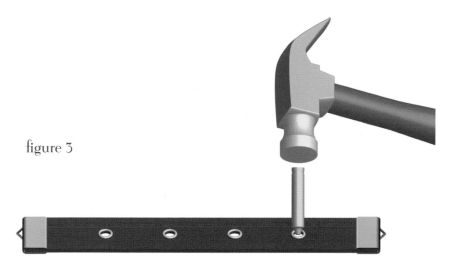

figure 3

8. Face two connectors back-to-back.

9. Open one jump ring and attach three pearl dangles. Before closing, use the jump ring to connect to the first loops of the connectors on the three-loop side. Repeat to connect dangles to the third loops of the connectors. Open one jump ring and attach the locket. Before closing, use the jump ring to connect to the second loops of the connectors (**figure 4**).

10. Use one jump ring to attach the one-loop side of the connectors to one ribbon crimp.

11. Face the remaining two connectors back-to-back.

12. Open one jump ring and attach the D ring along the flat side to the first loops of the connectors on the three-loop side. Repeat to connect the D ring to the second and third loops.

13. Use one jump ring to attach the one-loop side of the connectors to the open ribbon crimp (**figure 5**).

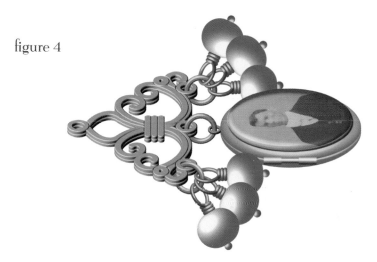

figure 4

figure 5

Gallery of Steampunk
DESIGNS

Steampunk Ring

Daniel Proulx, Catherinette Rings.
Brass, copper, seraphinite. 2008

Photo: Daniel Proulx

Photo: Ricky Wolbrom

Handmade Steampunk Unisex and Diverse Vintage Neo-Victorian Jewelry

EDM Designs, Ricky Wolbrom.
Found objects, brass, sterling silver.

Photo: Libby Bulloff

Dulcet

Annie Singer.
Brass, found objects, and quartz.

Photo: Ted Singer

Vacuum Tube Jewelry

Libby Bulloff.
Vacuum tubes, wire, rubber.

Photo: Julia DeVille

Mechanical Wing.

Julie DeVille.
Feathers, sterling silver.

Photo: Seth Tice-Lewis

Photo: Seth Tice-Lewis

Revisiting the Small Town
of Childhood. (& detail)

Madelyn Smoak.
Mixed metals diadem with etched brass,
found objects, tintypes, crystals, and resin.

Photo: Ricky Wolbrom

Handmade Steampunk Unisex and Diverse Vintage Neo-Victorian Jewelry

EDM Designs by Ricky Wolbrom.
Found objects, brass, sterling silver.

Photo: Ricky Wolbrom

Photo: Subversive Jewelry

Cameo Wreath Necklace

Subversive Jewelry by Justin Giunta.
Ruby crystal brooches, cameo brooch,
eagle detail, chain.

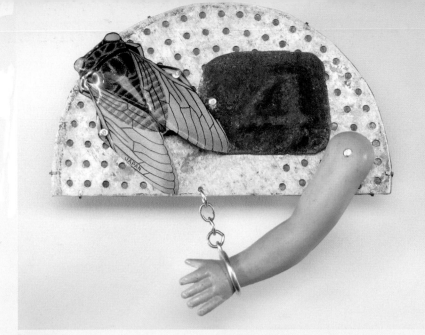

Photo: Bob Ebendorf

Cicada 1

Bob Ebendorf.
Mixed media, found parts, aluminum, tin, found metal, doll arm.

Claws and Roses

Bob Ebendorf.
Mixed media, green beach glass, 24K gold, crab claw, plastic, silver.

Photo: Subversive Jewelry

Photo: Bob Ebendorf

Wood and Rhinestone Ball Necklace

Subversive Jewelry by Justin Giunta.
Wooden balls and rhinestone brooches on assorted blackened chains.

Lava Stone Dark Moon Necklace

Subversive Jewelry by Justin Giunta.
Vintage box chain, hex beads, lava beads.

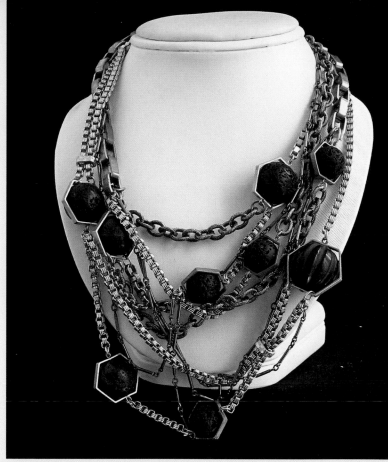

And She Road a Horse Named Whistler

Brenda Schweder.
Vintage cowgirl toy, boat swain pipe, iron wire, leather bible cover, horsehair, brass chain, linen.

Cog Bracelet

Atomefabrik by Nicolas Chambon.
Fabricated brass.

Hinged Copper Lockets

Richard Salley.
Steel washers, iron wire, copper,
leather, photograph.

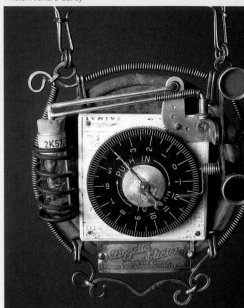

Early Incubator

Richard Salley.
Rusted steel lid, iron wire, copper
wire, clock parts, typewriter keys,
Faux Bone, glass bottle, wasp.

Uncle Julie Says Goodnight

Jean Campbell.
Watch parts, D rings, jump rings, eyelets,
seed beads, shoe liner, paper.

Pearls of Time

Cynthia Deis.
Pearls, watch face, copper chain,
brass filigree, brass findings.

Gear Bracelet

Richard Salley.
Found steel cabinet hinge, etched copper,
iron wire, brass clock gear segment,
costume pearl, leather.

My Heart Soars

Richard Salley.
Iron wire, sterling silver, etched brass,
copper, steel washer, brass watch segment.

List of Artists

Melanie Brooks is a porcelain bead maker and jewelry designer who sells her work through her website www.earthenwoodstudio.com. Melanie creates a variety of porcelain beads in unusual styles inspired by many alternative- and punk-related genres. Melanie has developed a line of porcelain bead components based on images and impressions from her favorite Steampunk films.

Cynthia Deis, owner of the bead stores Ornamentea and Panopolie in Raleigh, North Carolina, has been working with tiny things and found objects since childhood, when she tied washers to a charm bracelet with yellow ribbon. She has designed jewelry for major clients and is the author of *Beading With Filigree* (Lark Books, 2008). Cynthia teaches in her bead stores and creates new designs for her website www.beadfreak.com.

Jen Hilton is an artist and jewelry designer who lives in Raleigh, North Carolina. She is the founder and organizer of the Raleigh Jewelry Meetup Group at www.meetup.com/raleighjewelry/. Visit her website at www.JLHJewelry.com.

Jamie Hogsett is author of *Stringing Style* (Interweave Press, 2005) and coauthor of the Create Jewelry series of books published by Interweave Press. Jamie is the education coordinator for Soft Flex Company and a freelance editor and jewelry designer. She lives in Fort Collins, Colorado.

Barbe Saint John is a San Francisco–based mixed-media artist who envisions herself as a modern day alchemist/archeologist, transforming items that are broken, rusty, lost, sparkly, abandoned, or forgotten into new creations. These lovelies appear on her website, www.barbesaintjohn.com, and on her blog, barbesaintjohn.blogspot.com.

Jane Mormino was born and raised in Charlotte, North Carolina. She's an expert wordsmith and self-taught artist who creates striking jewelry carefully crafted from a love of etymology, ingenuity, and tiny, tiny things. Inspired by melodic meaning and hidden beauty, Jane infuses a delicate aesthetic with a thinking-woman's level of detail that has earned her critical acclaim from clients all over the world. Her works have been commissioned in Germany and Hong Kong and are sold via her etsy shops Ergane and Fearlessfreak, local art shows, and private commissions from her studio in the heart of downtown Cary, North Carolina.

Margot Potter, The Impatient Crafter, is a mixed-media jewelry and craft artist, best-selling author, freelance designer, internationally popular blogger, TV host, consultant, viral marketing expert, and crafty gal about town. You can visit Margot's world and access her books, her award-winning videos, her portfolio, and her blog at www.margotpotter.com.

Annie Singer has applied her unique vision and talent to many fields, including drafting, illustrating children's books and botanical science publications, designing logos and signage, sewing clothing and costumes, and assembling mixed-media and textile art pieces. She has teaching experience in poster making, beading, herb and cooking classes, and swimming. Annie has a B.A. in art from College Misericordia in Dallas, Pennsylvania. She has two grown children and lives with her husband in the Minneapolis area of Minnesota.

Madelyn Smoak is an award-winning metalsmith/jeweler whose work encompasses everything from Steampunk and found-object jewelry to fabricated crowns. You can find her work on the Web at http://MadArtjewelry.etsy.com.

Tracy Thomasson has been making jewelry for more than five years and has been crafting all of her life. She currently resides in Cary, North Carolina, where she lives with her husband, two cats, and way too many beads. You can find more of her creations online at thomcatdesigns.etsy.com or email her with any questions at thomcatdesigns@gmail.com.

Andrew Thornton is a Brooklyn-based fine artist, specializing in painting and collage. His works are in private collections around the globe. He also works part-time with his family at Green Girl Studios, www.greengirlstudios.com. Visit his blog at http://andrew-thornton.blogspot.com/.

Jean Yates lives with her husband Jim and her family in Westchester, New York. Two of their sons are autistic, and Jean and Jim feel this circumstance has affected their life in every way, changing it to something far more special than they might have foreseen. She is author of the jewelry book *Links: Inspired Bead* and *Wire Jewelry Creations* (North Light Books, 2007). Read her blog at http://prettykittydogmoonjewelry.blogspot.com/.

Credits

Abney Park;
www.abneypark.com

Apsara;
www.tomsepe.com/apsara/home.htm

Richard Borge, illustrator/animator;
www.richardborge.com

Greg Broadmore;
Weta Workshop; www.wetanz.com

Melanie Brooks, Earthenwood Studio;
www.earthenwoodstudio.com

Libby Bulloff, Exoskeleton Cabaret,
www.exoskeletoncabaret.com

Nicolas Chambon, Atomefabrik;
www.atomefabrik.com

Clockwork Cabaret;
www.clockworkcabaret.com

Holly Conrad, costumer;
www.fyriel.com

Cynthia Deis, Ornamentea;
www.ornamentea.com, www.beadfreak.com

Julia DeVille, artist;
www.juliadeville.com

Kim Lee Dye, Topsy Turvy Design;
www.topsyturvydesign.com

Bob Ebendorf, artist

Kaja and Phil Foglio, Studio Foglio;
www.studiofoglio.com

Justin Guinta, Subversive Jewelry;
www.subversivejewelry.com

Stephane Halleux, artist;
www.stephanehalleux.com

Jen Hilton, Monkeyshines Beadery;
www.JLHJewelry.com

Guy Himber, V&A Steamworks;
www.flickr.com/photos/32482342@N05/

Jamie Hogsett, Soft Flex Company;
www.softflexcompany.com,
www.jamiehogsett.com

Aaron Ijams, Hexonal;
www.hexonal.deviantart.com/gallery/
?4363368#SteamPunk

Gina Kamentsky, artist;
www.ginakamentsky.com

La Carmina;
www.lacarmina.com

Jane McGregor Hamilton Mormino, Ergane;
www.ergane.etsy.com

Keith Newstead, artist;
www.keithnewsteadautomata.com

New York Couture;
www.newyorkcouture.net

Shannon O'Hare, Academy of Unnatural
Sciences;
www.neverwashaul.com

Margot Potter, The Impatient Crafter;
www.margotpotter.com

Rob Powell, artist;
www.robpowell.deviantart.com

Daniel Proulx, Catherinette Rings;
catherinetterings.etsy.com

Barbe Saint John, artist;
www.barbesaintjohn.com

Richard Salley, artist;
www.rsalley.com

Brenda Schweder, artist;
www.brendaschweder.com

Tom Sepe, artist;
www.tomsepe.com

Annie Singer, artist

Jake Von Slatt, The Steampunk Workshop;
www.steampunkworkshop.com

Madelyn Smoak, MadArt Jewelry;
www.MadArtjewelry.etsy.com

Steamcon;
www.steam-con.com

Steampunk Magazine;
www.steampunkmagazine.com

Tracy Thomasson, Thomcat Designs;
www.thomcatdesigns.etsy.com

Andrew Thornton, artist;
www.greengirlstudios.com,
www.andrew-thornton.blogspot.com/

Unextraordinary Gentlemen;
www.unextraordinarygentlemen.com

Vernian Process;
www.movementproductions.net/vernianprocess.html

Andrew Waser, Xylocopa Design;
www.xylocopa.com

Ricky Wolbrom, EDM Designs;
edmdesigns.etsy.com

Jean Yates, artist;
www.prettykittydogmoonjewelry.blogspot.com/

Supplies

Filigree Gears Necklace All supplies: Ornamentea (ornamentea.com).

The Anachronist Necklace Chain and bird charm: Blue Moon Beads (bluemoonbeads. com); findings: Beadalon (beadalon.com); glass bottle, watch fob, watch face, brass hook and watch parts: Ornamentea (ornamentea. com); Grungeboard, trinkets and fragments, Tim Holtz inks, Stickles, paint dabber, and applicators: Ranger (rangerink.com); vintage images and old book pages: ArtChix Studio (artchixstudio.com); metallic heart: Earthenwood Studio (earthenwoodstudio.com); skeleton key and compass heart: Green Girl Studios (greengirlstudios.com); scrolled wooden charm: Fusion Beads (fusionbeads. com); crystals, keishi pearls: Stone International; chipboard circle: Bazzill Basics (bazzillbasics.com); flourish and harlequin stamps: Inkadinkado (inkadinkado.com); Italian letter stamp: Hero Arts (heroarts.com); Mod Podge Plaid, UHU Saunders Manufacturing; milagros: Sacred Kitsch Studios (sacredkitschstudios.com).

Captured Time Ring Dark annealed wire: Ace Hardware stores (acehardware.com).

Love's Labour's Lost Necklace Chain: Blue Moon Beads (bluemoonbeads.com); frosted tubes and pearls: Great Craft Works (greatcraftworks.com); porcelain: Earthenwood Studio (earthenwoodstudio.com); key: Ornamentea (ornamentea.com); Bird charm: Green Girl Studios (greengirlstudios.com); Findings and wire: Beadalon (beadalon.com).

Gearrings Filigree: Ornamentea (ornamentea.com); head pins: Rings and Things (Rings-Things.com).

Minerva's Folly Cuff Cuff bracelet form: North Shore Vintage Findings (northshorevintagefindings.com); mini bolts and nuts: Objects and Elements (objectsandelements.com).

Portal Explorer's Necklace Check rings, conduits, primer: Home Depot (homedepot. com); brass brads: Office Depot (officedepot. com); floral gems, Stazon, Mod Podge: Michael's Crafts (michaels.com); melon beads, chain, findings, E-6000: The Bead Monkey (thebeadmonkey.com).

Time Traveler's Necklace Silver toggle and pewter ring and tube: Green Girl Studios (greengirlstudios.com); crimps and Swarovski crystal rondelles: Fusion Beads (fusionbeads. com); Vintaj natural brass butterfly filigree, jump rings, and figure eight links: Vintaj (vintaj. com); chain, watch face, watch cogs, vintage key, and adhesive: Ornamentea (ornamentea. com); pyrite, vintage German bumpy sugar glass rounds, and pewter daisy spacers: Talisman Associates (talismanbeads.com); vintage Egyptian crystal faceted drops: Bead and Rocks (beadsandrocks.com); decorative bronze ring: Ashes to Beauty Adornments (ashes2beauty.com).

White Star Line Necklace All supplies except stamps: Ornamentea (ornamentea.com).

Steam Voyageur Necklace Focal pendant: Kate McKinnon (KateMcKinnon.com); porcelain: Earthenwood Studio (earthenwoodstudio.com); heishi, bullet dangles: Objects and Elements (objectsandelements.com); rondelles, wire: Fusion Beads (fusionbeads.com); chain, findings: Art Beads (artbeads.com).

Machinery in Motion Necklace Porcelain: Earthenwood Studio (earthenwoodstudio.com); tiny brass dangles: Metalliferous (metalliferous. com); all other supplies: Fusion Beads (fusionbeads.com).

Horological Faery Gadget Necklace Goddess Charm: Fire Mountain Gems (firemountaingems.com).

Dirigible Aviatrix Necklace Bolts and nuts: Objects and Elements (objectsandelements. com) and Volcano Arts (volcanoarts.biz/); drill bits: hardware stores and Rio Grande (riogrande.com); mini compass: Manto Fev (mantofev.com); mica tile: U.S. Art Quest (usartquest.com/mica.htm); brass eyelets: Volcano Arts (volcanoarts.biz).

Voluminating Exhalator Bracelet Wire, Twist 'n' Curl mini set, WigJig Olympus-Lite, WigJig Spiral Maker Plus: Soft Flex Company (softflexcompany.com); brass pendants, beads, and findings: Vintaj Natural Brass, Co. (vintaj.com).

Tick Tock Drops Earrings Porcelain: Earthenwood Studio (earthenwoodstudio.com); clock hands: Klockit (klockit.com); all other supplies: Fusion Beads (fusionbeads.com).

Tempus Fugit Pendant All supplies: Ornamentea (ornamentea.com).

Admiral's Secret Cuff Locket, glass cabochon: Ornamentea (ornamentea.com); filigree: Ornamental Resources (ornamentalresources. com); leather, eyelets, D ring, ribbon ends: Michael's Crafts (michaels.com)